In That Number

Regan Burke

In That Number

One Woman's March

From the Streets of Protest to the Halls of Power

(And Beyond)

Regan Burke

TORTOISE BOOKS

CHICAGO, IL

FIRST EDITION, October 2020

©2020 Regan Burke

Published in the United States by Tortoise Books. www.tortoisebooks.com

ISBN-13: 978-1-948954-12-9

This book is a work of memoir, and is drawn from the author's experience, various artifacts and photographs, and recollections going back to an early age. Dialogue is approximate and appears in quotation marks for the benefit of the reader.

Cover image contains a photograph from the official White House photographer, Robert McNeely, that is in the public domain. Cover concept and design by Gerald Brennan. Cover photography by Joel Wintermantle. Cover Copyright ©2020 by Tortoise Books

Text includes a quote from "Christus Paradox" by Sylvia Dunstan, Copyright © 1991, GIA Publications, Inc.

Tortoise Books Logo Copyright ©2020 by Tortoise Books. Original artwork by Rachele O'Hare.

Introduction

In my fifties I was diagnosed with osteoarthritis and a mysterious pain condition, fibromyalgia. Joint replacement cured the arthritis in my knees and shoulder, but the surging episodic pain of fibromyalgia, arthritis in my back, and attendant insomnia remained. Since I have a history of drug addiction I couldn't risk prescription painkillers. Mindfulness meditation and *feldenkrais* (moving meditation) added enough of a reprieve from daily back pain to give me hope.

Hope also led me to Dr. John Stracks at Northwestern's Osher Center for Integrative Medicine. At my first visit Dr. Stracks pried my mind open enough for me to accept that emotions were a factor in painful physical symptoms like mine. His remedy? Writing. Writing? Yes, writing.

He recommended Dr. Howard Schubiner's workbook, *Unlearn Your Pain.* The barbed-wire suffering I experienced while writing down emotionally charged memories, evoked by the book's writing exercises, made me a believer. There's no doubt the connection between the mind and the body is real. At the completion of each writing exercise, I experienced a whoosh of pain relief.

I kept that whoosh going by enrolling in memoir writing classes. Initially, I hesitated to expose embarrassing episodes from my life to strangers. But this was my therapy, my bibliotherapy, and I had to tell deep truths for it to work. Beth Finke and Linda Miller, the best writing teachers I could ever have hoped for, have been extraordinarily helpful in keeping me on the road that leads to the truth.

Along the way, I ran into Kevin Coval, author of A *People's History of Chicago* and creative director at Young Chicago Authors. How could I write in prose the kind of truth he tells in his poetry? He invited me to the poetry writing workshops at YCA. I thought I'd be an observer but found myself participating. Kevin's work with young poets (who recite hard truths from the stages of *Louder Than a Bomb* poetry slams) made me realize I wouldn't die if I wrote my story out loud, in a book.

I'm an unabashed American. I have a curious and insatiable need to indulge in the freedoms guaranteed in the U.S. Constitution—to not only assemble publicly, but also express myself openly. Sometimes it's in the streets. Sometimes it's in Alcoholics Anonymous. Whenever and wherever the saints go marching, I want to be in that number.

Disclaimer

These are my memories. I strive for demonstrated, not autobiographical truth. I concede various illegal hypnotic drugs may have marred some memories. Nonetheless, the parade of stories is true. Some names have been altered to maintain personal privacy.

I owe not only my sobriety, but my life, to Alcoholics Anonymous. Yet I claim no personal distinction in AA. I do not represent Alcoholics Anonymous, nor am I a spokesperson or leader in the fellowship. Alcoholics Anonymous neither endorses nor opposes this writing.

Publisher's Note

The publisher would like to add that Alcoholics Anonymous is, quite deliberately, a non-political organization—born in the aftermath of America's failed attempt to use national politics as a means to eliminate alcoholism in the individual. The organization's founders realized (sensibly, in the publisher's opinion) that any organization that sought to provide relief to the suffering alcoholic needed to studiously avoid any involvement in political matters. It is our firm hope that, whatever your political affiliation, you will enjoy this story of one woman's journey—and that, if you do suffer from the disease of alcoholism, you will find a healthy respite.

Prologue

Fiction is obliged to stick to possibilities; Truth isn't. — *Mark Twain*

I hopped on the #3 bus at Chicago and Michigan Avenues having no clue when to pull the cord for the Wintrust Arena. It was 7:30 A.M., too early for rush hour. But people dressed in their finest kept boarding at every stop as we moved on down the avenue, and there was no mistaking when we got there. The cross streets swarmed with jaywalkers, Uber riders, taxi passengers, bus trippers, policemen, VIPs, and carpoolers teeming out of the parking garages. Parades of citizens streamed toward the entrances, lining up for the eight o'clock opening. Volunteers in blue "Bring In The Light" t-shirts hoisted colossal signs pointing to the ADA entrances. Others greeted people with disabilities at the curb.

"What's going on?" asked the bus driver.

"Lori Lightfoot's Inauguration," I said.

"Oh! The new mayor! Great day. End of the Chicago Machine."

Inside the arena, old friends who'd fought entrenched politicians for decades worked the event. Hi, Regan! Hi! Hi! Victorious voices all around; they directed me to two seats on the basketball court, eight rows from the stage. The Daley clan, who personified old-style Chicago politics, took their seats behind me. Powerless to stop the joy from the crowd who'd upended their well-oiled machine.

A familiar Chicago policeman came running over to say hello. Matthew Baio and I have known each other since we both worked for Illinois House Speaker Michael Madigan in the late 80s. Matt's official post was guarding the inside entrance of City Hall. We still saw each other every time I marched into the building protesting the previous mayors, or bought a dog license, or renewed my senior bus pass. I greeted him laughing, anticipating he'd be tickled about the new mayor.

"Matt, I just finished writing a memoir, and you're in it!" I said.

"What? No way! Is it about the time you asked me to be Bill Clinton's driver?"

"It is!" We had a riotous conversation reliving the scene from the March 1992 Illinois presidential primary: Matt, the silent navigator at the wheel, while George Stephanopoulos, James Carville, and Bruce Lindsey counseled Bill Clinton in the back.

My friend Peter arrived at the arena via train and bus from the far southwest side. A security guard said he was ticketed for the bleachers, not the floor, and prevented him from joining me. As it turned out, I was also ticketed for the bleachers—I had been inadvertently led to the VIP seats. I eyeballed Officer Baio, who'd moved to the other side of the court. But after a brief kerfuffle, and some walkie-talkie murmuring by the security guard, Peter and I found ourselves at last in the prized floor seats. Reverend Jesse Jackson's bodyguard sat down next to us, keeping eyes on his famous boss, one row ahead.

After the politicians paraded onto the stage and took their seats, the diminutive powerhouse, Lori Lightfoot, was sworn in. Then she took the microphone. The articulation of her vision for Chicago hit every issue. And right smack in the middle of her speech she highlighted a fear I'd expressed to her several times during the campaign.

"I'm looking ahead to a city where people want to grow old, and not flee," she said. "A city that is affordable for families and seniors."

Was it because we were so close to the stage that Peter and I felt like she was speaking directly to us? Would we still have sighed with relief if we'd been in the bleachers? I don't know. But I do know that it still pays to be friends with the right people in Chicago.

Chapter 1

In December 1942, my grandfather loaded two sons, two daughters and one trunk containing my mother's full-length wedding dress onto a train headed down to Key West. My mother's older sister Jean was staying behind in New Jersey, but the rest of the Ryan family was making the day-and-a-half trip to watch my mother Agnes get married to my father, William Lawrence Patrick Burke, a naval aviator. Agnes and Bill married under the buccaneer palms of St. Mary Star of the Sea Catholic Church. Ernest Hemingway's sons supposedly served as altar boys for the Mass. My father had no family in attendance.

(When Bill had registered for the draft two years earlier, he'd listed my mother as his next-of-kin, a term usually reserved for a blood relative or a spouse. They'd been loving each other since their early college years, long before they were married, and he already thought of her as his closest contact in case of emergency.)

With no children to mind, the newlyweds spent evenings in the Officer's Club chattering about the day's news over rum and cigars flown in from Cuba. The young men were aviators, gunners and radiomen—crews from the shiny new Grumman Avenger torpedo bombers that were rolling off the assembly lines in those early war years. Some were Naval intelligence. Some worked in the OSS, the precursor to the CIA. The women were all wives and girlfriends. Anyone who didn't drink was not to be trusted. They prided themselves on never going to restaurants, nor any gathering, party, picnic or church function, unless they knew alcohol would be served.

The earliest known ugly secret in my family is that my mother was drunk in the Georgetown Inn in Washington with my father when her mother died. She wasn't located until the next day. Their married life began with Bill spending two weeks in the brig after a drunken brawl over Agnes with other men in the Officers Club.

The word "alcoholism" wasn't widely used in those days. Alcoholics were bums on the Bowery, certainly not members of the credentialed class. No one ever mentioned alcoholic relatives. Most large Irish Catholic families had an alcoholic or two who disappeared into the country's underbelly, wiping their existence out of family memories.

I've caught glimpses of my parents in those years through letters and photographs, trying, as perhaps all children do, to understand them. One letter from my mother—stamped Key West, 1943, and addressed to her sister Jean in New Jersey—started off as follows:

"Dearest Jean, As long as you've seen my good stationery, I've decided to use this stuff. Laziness accounts for all the weeks I haven't written."

In the letter, my mother gossiped about former classmates. Dorothy Castle's husband Ed was in the Navy's Sound School training to detect enemy submarines; he'd soon be commanding a sub chaser. "Water Wings Haley, up in Miami, was waiting for a ship to get outfitted that he would command."

She mentioned that my father "will jump from Ensign to full Lt. if the Air Corps ever gets around to promotions." Then she wrote, "I personally don't give a damn, but that's all anyone talks about."

Ah-ha! There's the mother I knew—not giving a damn.

She casually revealed that my father's mission, patrolling the Florida Straits between Key West and Cuba for German submarines, was a military secret. She also told how my father and his fellow crewmembers would smuggle in contraband they'd acquired on liberty in Cuba—English gabardine, cigars and liquor.

"We've become quite the rum and scotch ring. I've had to acquire a taste for Daiquiris because of the lack of gin," she wrote.

Next we read about her new bathing suit, her tan, the new officers' club where "we have to bring in our own liquor because it's on an Army Reservation."

I'd always known her to have a devil-may-care attitude about matters of propriety and legality, and I'd always thought that had come to her by way of my father. But my mother's own words betrayed her—she had fun cheating and smuggling. It was as much a part of her as clothes, shopping, or mixing a gin and tonic.

How had she become so nonchalant toward lawlessness? She'd grown up in a normal house, the second child of seven, all of whom revered their successful attorney father and adoring mother. She'd studied at Georgetown Visitation College, an all-female convent school on the grounds of Georgetown University. (It was where she and Jean both met their husbands.) Yet, like my father, she wasn't governed by her conscience.

Two of my sisters and I were born in Annapolis immediately after World War II. By then, my father was stationed at the Naval Academy, where he defended Naval personnel on trial for petty theft and black market racketeering. At night he drove the hour-long commute back and forth to Georgetown Law School to complete his final year.

Upon entering the District of Columbia Bar, he moved us to a Georgetown townhouse and began his civilian law career. Powerful union boss John L. Lewis hired him as general counsel to the United Mine Workers of America. They held the same liberal political views but Lewis, a devout Mormon, and my father, a binge-drinker already in the early stages of alcoholism, had battling temperaments. Lewis put his alcohol intolerance on hold long enough to let my father write and implement the landmark UMWA 1950 Pension Plan, the first retirement benefits ever negotiated for American labor.

The backyard of our Georgetown townhouse abutted the garden of a young senator from Massachusetts, John F. Kennedy. After my father's first few successful years, we moved to a five-bedroom brick colonial at the corner of Fox Hall Road and Edmunds Street in Northwest Washington. Both of my parents had friends and relatives living, working and matriculating in the District. They all found an open door at our house. I never knew who would be joining my sisters and me at the breakfast table, or who'd be passed out on the living room couch after an all-night party. No one ever cared where their cigarette ashes landed, or bothered to clean up spilled drinks.

No one ever told us we were Democrats. Neither of my parents campaigned, nor wore political buttons, nor wrote thoughtful letters to politicians. They were Catholics, went to Catholic schools and colleges, and married in the Catholic church. They took on the mantle of Irish Catholicism as if it were a physical birthmark, a once-a-Catholic-always-a-Catholic mental tattoo unaccompanied by belief in God or Jesus. They took advantage of the culture of the sacraments—Holy Communion, Marriage, Baptism—as an excuse to have parties.

They argued. About money, mostly. And other women, other men. They agreed on important things: for instance, Pope Pius XII was a backwater imbecile for invoking papal infallibility in 1950 when he proclaimed all Catholics must believe Mary didn't suffer physical death and was assumed into heaven. This new doctrine, along with the Pope's behavior during the Holocaust (insisting the Church of Rome stay neutral), drove them away from any real observance of the faith.

They hated right-wing bullies like Senator Joseph McCarthy and J. Edgar Hoover. McCarthy ruined lives with his public witch hunts and unsubstantiated accusations against communist sympathizers. He chaired the House Un-American Activities Committee (HUAC)—my earliest television memories besides *I Love Lucy*. FBI Director Hoover amassed power by steering favorable press and policy his way using his secret files to blackmail congressmen and presidents alike. When my parents watched the HUAC hearings, they were keeping an eye out for people they knew—friends who worked on congressional staffs, or were being investigated, or had been recruited to spy on others.

Throughout their lives my parents derided the Red Cross for raising wartime money for the troops, then charging soldiers and sailors for giveaways like toothpaste, coffee and donuts. My mother eagerly showed how smart she was in these matters. After all, she'd attended college. Gossiping about under-informed conversationalists, she'd shriek, "What do you expect? They don't even read *The New York Times!*"

They excoriated any friend or relative who stopped drinking. A reformed drunk—those were dirty words. With all their strong opinions about religion and politics, their knowledge of Washington policies and personalities, and their war experiences, the foundational belief of my parents was that life without alcohol was as unsophisticated and tasteless as a Jersey Shore diner.

"Say in a loud voice 'My name is Regan and it's from Shakespeare,'" my mother instructed me when I was about three years old. It was my answer to the universal question I'd get from strangers: "Where did that name come from?" My name was a bit odd in the John-and-Mary fifties, and Agnes abhorred conversations about children, especially her own. Swapping motherly stories ranked high on her long and unforgiving list of things to avoid in social settings. She loved my name, hated talking about it.

Catholics were required to name their children after saints whose virtues the child would learn and emulate throughout life. My parents, particularly Agnes, disdained this convention. The parish priest in Annapolis called me "Regina" at my baptism, the Latin version of Regan. Regina, an approved Catholic name, was short for *Regina Caeli*: Queen of Heaven, mother of Jesus, and queen of every creature. Regina Caeli, with her unblemished reputation, was a stark contrast to Shakespeare's Regan.

In *King Lear*, Regan is the king's middle daughter. She is a power-hungry evil sister who tries to flatter her father into giving her all the family fortune, then drives him out into a raging storm. (Shakespeare's metaphor for insanity.) In the end, Regan's jealous older sister poisons her.

Of course, my father was no king.

Bill Burke and his two sisters, Kathleen and Mary Margaret, lost their mother, Katherine Kilroy Burke, when they were toddlers in Terre Haute, Indiana. The motherless Burke children moved into the Kilroy family home with their maternal grandparents, seven aunts, and two uncles. In the early twentieth century, Terre Haute, a railroad town on the Wabash River, sat in the largest coal-producing county in the US. The crossroads entertainment included beer halls full of hustlers, alcoholics, floozies, grifters, drifters, desperadoes, and high-stakes gamblers. Bill's father, William A. Burke, traveled as a railroad worker on the Louisiana and Nashville line, often coming into Terre Haute at dawn, visiting his children for a few hours, and hopping back on the afternoon train. It's been said he'd been secretly organizing railroad workers for the American Federation of Labor and had to be careful where he laid his head for fear of the anti-union thugs hired by the railroad. (These were the years leading up to the passage of the Railway Labor Act of 1926, which required employers to allow collective bargaining, and not to discriminate against their employees for joining a union.)

The Kilroy aunts, restrained by Catholic mores, stayed out of the beer halls. They succumbed to the river town's unbridled ethos though, sitting on the front porch of their three-story Victorian, playing cards day and night, welcoming friends and strangers alike to come on up, have a seat, throw a few in the till, and deal a hand. The aunts capitalized on young Bill's natural charm and intelligence by turning him into their little card sharp. They taught their precocious young prodigy to gather personal information about their marks and use it to lure them into higher stakes games. *C'mon, mister, when you win you can buy your wife a diamond ring.*

One of the aunts, Sister Mary Agnes (a Dominican nun at St. Ceceilia's Convent in Nashville) worried her Billy wouldn't get to college if he stayed around Terre Haute. A confidante to patrons and families of the all-girls' school at St. Cecelia's, Sister Mary Agnes persuaded a wealthy socialite to pay for her nephew Billy to attend a year at a military school. She hastily arranged for the high school football star to say goodbye to Terre Haute and board the train for Nashville. He walked from the train station to the Cain-Sloan department store for his first suit and wing tips. Then he overnighted in the convent's boys orphanage (where he'd spent grade school summers) before heading out for the

Massanutten Military Academy in the Shenandoah Mountains of Virginia. Georgetown University awarded him a four-year football scholarship, and eventually hired him to coach football during law school before he joined the Navy. Sister Mary Agnes was certain she'd rescued her Billy from the ne'er-do-well Terre Haute Kilroys and river-town temptations.

While he was at school, Bill earned spending money in all-night bridge games. His permanent bridge partner was a mysterious older woman who sent her chauffered limousine to his dorm on Friday evenings and delivered him back Saturday morning. So much for avoiding temptation.

During the year I was supposed to be in the first grade, I contracted all the childhood diseases—measles, chicken pox, mumps—and missed most of the school year. The household regulars, who always seemed to have a beer in one hand and a cigarette in the other, told me not to worry about school because, as smart as I was, the nuns couldn't teach me anything I didn't already know. I believed them.

One of my parents' friends lived in the attic. I know he came out at night, because all the adults told morning-after stories in which he figured prominently. I finally came upon him one morning in the kitchen. He was guzzling a bottle of orange juice standing in front of the open ice box wearing a buttoned-up wrinkled trench coat and loafers. No socks, bare legs.

"Hi, I'm Ted," he said.

"Hi. I'm Regan. It's from Shakespeare."

"Well, what's your favorite thing to do, Regan?"

"I like monkeys."

"Want to go to the zoo?"

"Yes!"

"Ok, get your sisters and get in the car."

Ted had no car. He meant my mother's car. The keys were always in the ignition.

We drove down Fox Hall Road toward the Washington National Zoo, and promptly crashed into a telephone pole. No one was hurt. My father represented Ted in court. Charges were dismissed, but Ted was required to pay for the telephone pole.

"Your honor, I have no funds and no income," he proclaimed. "I live off the bounty of my friends."

Ted would have gone to jail had my father not forked over the cash. My parents howled over this incident for all the rest of their days. All their friends loved re-telling the story. There was never mention of the danger to the three little girls in the back seat.

That house, that job, and those glory years were the only things my parents would ever brag about. They were living the dream, and they lived back into the dream as time went on, forever grasping at their dressed-up past. Meanwhile alcohol was destroying the dream.

Chapter 2

Whatever possessed my mother to force me to sit at a plate of uneaten lima beans for hours? Did the doctors tell her that children needed to eat their vegetables, come hell or high water? Or was it something she'd decided on her own, some ritual of conformance and obedience? When I put the light green kidney shape in my mouth, my tongue moved it to my baby molars, gingerly munching up and down, side to side, until I felt the mushy bean pop out of the slimy skin onto my tongue. I gasped, and my reflexive inhale involuntarily pulled the glob to the back of my throat. I gagged on the paper-like skin, exhaling the sodden lump back through the front of my teeth and out onto my plate.

"You eat those lima beans," she said. Sick and exhausted, my young body just sat there, ignoring the directive. After everyone went to bed, I dumped the loathsome things in the garbage. That night I vowed to forever hate lima beans. It was an early indication of what would become my unyielding, uncompromising, black-and-white view of life.

(Granted, we all hated vegetables. My older sister would feign putting a forkful of beans in her mouth; she exuded an air of superiority, showing early signs of the competitive streak that's never been pruned. Meanwhile my younger sister figured out how to put hers in a neat pocket formed by her napkin; she'd dump it in the trash while no one was looking. And that's been her coping mechanism throughout life: hiding unpleasant situations.)

My mother shook me awake early one morning on my fourth or fifth birthday. Men were waiting downstairs to wallpaper and paint. This was my birthday present—new wallpaper. I had to quickly get dressed and stay out of my room until they were finished.

"C'mon, we'll get your sisters and go visit Joanne!"

My mother's youngest sister lived in the Maryland countryside about an hour from our home in Washington. She must have been about 20. She attended Georgetown Visitation high school and junior college with the Smith girls, whose mother had inherited an eighteenth century Maryland estate, The Dower House, from socialite Cissy Patterson, owner of the *Washington Times-Herald*. During her school breaks, Joanne stayed at the Dower House, and the young women would spend those June days lounging around the pool in their swimsuits with their cigarettes and tanning lotion.

On this trip, my sisters and I all got our hair washed; we were set out in the sunshine to dry while my mother, Joanne, and the Smith girls painted their nails, gossiped, and laughed over cold beer in the estate's coach house.

My mother directed me to an oversized lounge chair near the shade of a mighty Southern Magnolia.

"Lay down there, Regan," she said, "and don't get up until your hair is dry."

I looked up into the old-growth tree bursting with sturdy white flowers that looked like folded linen. Sweet-smelling like the Smith girls. This is the first time I remember birds flying in and out of tree branches. The sun fell through the breeze into the dark fleshy leaves and lulled me into a meditative reverie that I can easily reconstruct whenever I'm under a summer tree, or any time I catch a whiff of magnolias.

At the close of day we returned home and I ran upstairs to my new room. Everything was covered in red roses—the walls, the ceiling, the bedspread, the pillows. It was the best birthday present I've ever received, and indeed, the only one I can remember from my childhood.

Within a year, my father's job, the house, and the rose-filled room had all gone south. We hid from creditors in hotels around Washington and the Jersey Shore, then moved in with my mother's father and stepmother without my father.

On the Atlantic City boardwalk at the start of that vagabond summer, I won a stuffed panda bear. He was big enough to cling to the side of my six-year-old body, but small enough for me to promenade with, and to swing him by one arm without touching the ground. In no time at all, he responded to my adoration by throwing his arms around my neck and telling me he loved me.

Neither of my two sisters won anything that day. This was pre-casino Atlantic City: a carnival of amusements and seaside pleasures along the boardwalk, a zoo of bourgeois tourists, high-falutin' hoi poloi, hawkers, and hucksters. As we strolled along, we were stopped by well-wishers congratulating me on my big prize. In my triumph I felt malicious satisfaction; meanwhile my sisters looked sideways at me, contemptuous.

My parents had us lodged seventy-five miles north of Atlantic City, in a boarding house above a restaurant in Sea Girt; my mother's sister Jean lived in town, in a large home with her husband and six children. Our fun-loving cousins entertained us at the beach all day and at their lively dinner table in the evening.

One day, my father told us we were going to attend the local Catholic school in September. He had us dress in our best ensembles and pull on our white cotton gloves, and he drove us to

St. Catherine-By-The-Sea to be presented to the authorizing priest. I left my prized panda safely tucked in bed.

My father, dressed in his seersucker suit, knit tie and two-toned wing-tips, pitched his story to the good man of God. He said he wanted to enroll the three of us in the church's grade school but was short of funds. Would Father So-And-So lend him the money for our school uniforms? My father promised to repay the church, and include a hefty contribution, as soon as his (fabricated) client, Senator John F. Kennedy, settled up for some legal fees. With the priest's check safely inside my father's leather wallet, we walked out of the church, slid into the station wagon, and returned to our boarding house.

As we wiggled out of the station wagon to change into our swimsuits, the proprietor greeted us on the sidewalk to tell us we were no longer welcome. Since he'd not been paid all summer, we were locked out; he'd keep our belongings until he received payment in full.

Our possessions were never seen again. My father disappeared with the check from the bamboozled priest.

The next thing I knew my mother, two sisters and I were living with my grandfather in north Jersey.

Adults in my life never tolerated outward displays of unhappiness. "Cut it out! Grow up," was my mother's common admonition whenever she caught me in tears. I had to moan privately every night for my panda, trapped in debtor's prison in a damp attic at the Shore. I gave no thought to other possessions, to where we'd go to school, or to my father's whereabouts. I still trusted grown-ups. And besides, I'd started paying attention at Sunday Mass. Jesus would watch over me. I had to believe it.

My sisters and I surreptitiously snickered at my grandfather and his wife for all the peculiar rules of their childless household.

We secretly dangled our fingers and toes in the goldfish pond in the backyard for hours, and played hide and seek with the neighborhood kids after dinner until the fireflies and mosquitoes sent us indoors.

My father appeared unexpectedly one day to take me to lunch. We drove thirty minutes into Manhattan to the garden restaurant on the lower plaza of Rockefeller Center. I knew about the Rockefeller Center Christmas tree and skating rink from *The Howdy Doody Show*, but I didn't know that that TV place had a summer life.

He greeted the *maitre d'* respectfully, handed over his straw hat, and introduced me by my name, instead of the usual, "This is my daughter." He politely asked for a table close to the outdoor plaza. He wanted us to imagine the rink full of winter skaters. The sun shone on the mammoth golden Prometheus statue across the plaza, gilding the mist rising from the roaring water of the fountain. He promised we'd come back, rent skates, and glide around under the famous Christmas tree.

The waiters acted like they knew him. His godly brown eyes softened into place as he read the menu. Alone with him, without my sisters and mother, I felt as beloved as Doodyville's Princess SummerFallWinterSpring.

He told me how proud he was that I'd learned to swim in the ocean that summer. He ordered drinks. When the waiter placed the frosty long stemmed cocktail glass full of gin and vermouth on the table, my father loosened up before he even took a sip. The cone-shaped bowl of clear liquid looked harmless. He consumed his martini before I was halfway through my Shirley Temple. I watched him through the empty glass as his eyes turned opaque, energetic, hair-raising. One eyebrow lifted and he yelled for another martini at a passing waiter, not ours. When the women lunching nearby said I was adorable, he started talking to them, ignoring me.

I sat completely alone. Like a hostage. Afraid I wouldn't get home. Mad at my mother. Why did she let me go with him? Where was Jesus? I have no idea what happened next, but one thing I've never forgotten: one martini turned my father into a monster.

I vowed to never drink one.

Chapter 3

Between rampaging binges, my father always managed to talk his way into a CEO's or union president's office where, after dropping names like John F. Kennedy or John L. Lewis, he'd secure large retainers. He'd perform his contractual obligations long enough to add legitimacy to his curriculum vitae. Then he'd succumb to his demons, drink round-the-clock, and walk out with the money. He often had to get out of town fast, leaving my mother with the job of packing and moving before the landlord caught us. His Clark Gable looks, baritone voice and masterful tongue worked to charm real estate agents and landlords into admitting us into homes in upper middle class neighborhoods, where shame resided in neither the outward society nor in my parents' inward consciousness. We were a family of grifters.

Somehow we ended up in Terre Haute. On the first day of the school year, the nun circled the room asking each new second grader to stand and state their name.

"Regan," I said.

"Well, that's not a saint's name. It must be a middle name. What is your first name?"

"Regan, it's from Shakespeare," I shuddered.

"How did you get baptized with that name?"

Having no knowledge of the Regina baptism, I froze in condemned fear and slid silently back into a doomed existence at my desk. I knew I was going to die and go straight to hell.

Next, each of us stood to read a sentence from our readers.

I rose, steadied my feet, stammered, shook and finally said, "I can't read."

A lot of commotion formed around this fact in the days following, some of which had to do with my baptismal name. But the inability to read at the beginning of the second grade seemed worse. I heard my parents tell people offhandedly it was because I was sick and out of school for so much of the first grade that I'd had to start school over.

"I had no idea she couldn't read," Agnes adroitly announced to the mother superior, deflecting any blame in the matter to my father. "He's the smart one—he was supposed to teach her."

But I knew the real reason I was deficient: I didn't have a saint's name.

I felt safe repeating the first grade because Gael, my younger sister, was in the first grade; she shielded me from shame, putting her arm around me and letting others know we were not only sisters, we were pals.

Since my original first grade in Washington was interrupted not only by my childhood illnesses, but also by my profligate parents, I didn't learn about the Holy Ghost until I got to the Terre Haute school. Casper the Friendly Ghost was also on my mind— the bubbly, happy, peaceable cartoon character who tried desperately to befriend humans because he was repulsed by his sinister fellow ghosts. When our nun taught the class about the three persons of the Trinity, I conflated the latter one with the ghost I'd seen on TV. The poor guy terrified most people, even though his spirit was warm-hearted and affable. Now he was one of the persons of God. And I needed Him.

My third-grade sister Maere ridiculed me relentlessly about flunking second grade. She did so in front of her friends—and in front of what would have been my friends, if she hadn't poisoned them against me. I prayed to Casper the Holy Ghost that he would scare Maere into leaving me alone. And for the most part, it worked.

I never had any trouble with the Trinity. Catholics bless themselves by making the sign of the cross, tapping the head, heart and each shoulder, while reciting "In the Name of the Father, the Son and the Holy Ghost." The concept of the Trinity was simple—three persons in one, like a cross. For the life of me I don't know why theologians are always trying to explain it. Perhaps they don't have Casper to guide them.

At Halloween I dressed as Casper. Agnes wasn't the least bit interested in dabbling in children's holidays, much less making costumes. But my Casper costume was a cinch. As long as I didn't cut holes for my eyes, she let me drape a white sheet over my head. Then Gael, in her hobo costume, led me around trick-or-treating. Maere, in her I-Love-Lucy outfit, called out to us when she passed us in the street—surrounded, as always, by a pack of friends.

"Look! Stupid costumes on stupid girls."

I started collecting *Casper the Friendly Ghost* comic books in 1952 when I was six. They survived four evictions—packing, storage, moving, and unpacking. By the time I was ten I had them stacked up alongside *Superman* comics in my closet. One day while I played dodgeball in the street with the neighborhood kids, Maere, who never cleaned our shared room, threw away my whole collection. She said it was time for me to grow up. The slick odor of those mistreated keepsakes haunted me for a time. But Casper's friendship and protection eventually evaporated.

About that time, Catholics started saying "Holy Spirit" instead of "Holy Ghost." The only image I had of the Holy Spirit was an inanimate white dove hanging open-winged over statues of Jesus. He certainly didn't look like he needed friends like Casper did. Unable to connect with Casper anymore, and having no idea what to do with the Holy Spirit, I slinked away from the entire trinitarian God.

By the time we moved to Terre Haute, television was brightening the lost hours of the day. TV watching was new enough in the fifties that no one ever spoke of limiting the time children viewed the black-and-white images jumping around inside the tiny box. Indeed, my parents used TV drama and comedy shows as a respite from the network news. Stalin, USSR, Iron Curtain, the Red Army, the Berlin Airlift, NATO, the CIA— these words blared out of the TV, put worry on adult faces, and terrified me. Then my sisters and I would gather on the floor to watch our favorite weekly shows—*Mickey Mouse, Roy Rogers, The Lone Ranger and Hopalong Cassidy*. It's one of the few communal activities I remember between us.

A weekly show, *I Love Lucy*, came into our lives in the early fifties. It starred Lucille Ball as Lucy, and her husband, Desi Arnaz, as Ricky Ricardo. The naïve, curious, ambitious, conniving and untalented I-Love-Lucy sought love and approval in show business, and schemed her way into crazy situations that led to trouble for her and Ricky, and for their friends, Fred and Ethel Mertz. At the end of each half-hour show, I-Love-Lucy was forgiven and everyone hugged. From the age of five through eleven, as long as we had a television, I never missed an episode. I-Love-Lucy had everything I wished for my mother—vitality, ambition, curiosity, best friends, fun costumes, and love for her family. And she didn't drink.

In 1954 my mother drove past the sixteen-hundred-seat Indiana Theater on Wabash Avenue in Terre Haute while my eight-year-old eyes peered out from the backseat. Parked curbside, an oversized flamingo-pink tractor trailer emblazoned with the words, "Long Long Trailer" promoted the new Lucille Ball-Desni Arnaz movie.

"You are not going to that movie!" my mother said, reading my mind.

(Agnes, like her sister, Jean, insisted it was not her job to provide entertainment for her children. Aunt Jean was the exact opposite of I-Love-Lucy. Whip-smart, well-informed and organized, her only ambition—to connect to Jersey Shore high society—led her to marry a charming, well-turned-out blue-blooded alcoholic with a dowry. Always the strongest, most graceful and best-dressed woman in the room, she wasn't prone to bumbling mishaps—until cocktail hour. She laughed with others, but the only lines she delivered herself were opinionated sarcastic put-downs of those who didn't meet her standards, a requirement in East-coast society. She had seven children and left them to entertain each other without her involvement.)

I-Love-Lucy was my first role model, the woman I wanted to imitate. The real-life women in my life—my mother, Jean, and the ever-present nuns—were opinionated and bossy, but never seemed happy or carefree. Though they had strong personalities, their worlds were ruled by men—husbands and priests. Not Lucy. She cooked up and executed fun adventures with her best friend despite her husband's admonitions and prohibitions. I anchored her example of life well-lived to my future subconscious. (As it happened, my later film role models were a little less wholesome—I learned everything I know about how to please men from Linda Lovelace in *Deep Throat*.)

★

In 1949 the Soviet Union had started the Cold War by detonating their first atomic bomb, blockading Berlin and pushing its way into Poland and Eastern Europe. The voices I'd heard swirling above my head at cocktail hour in our Washington home had told me the Russians wanted to rule the world and they were coming for us. Everyone acted like this was the worst thing that could ever happen.

Then air raid drills were concocted by the federal government through the National Civil Defense Administration to protect people from incoming A-bombs, even though common folk wisdom said only cockroaches would survive a nuclear attack. Teachers were required by law to conduct impromptu air raid drills by shouting, Drop!—a signal to school children to jump out of their seats, crawl under their desks, fall over their knees and cover their heads. The nuns at my schools added the instruction to recite Hail Marys aloud while on the floor.

"Holy Mary, Mother of God, pray for us sinners, now and at the hour of our death. Amen."

At seven, I didn't understand the difference between a drill and the real event and I went to my death every time I huddled under that desk. I feared the A-Bomb was the worst thing that could ever happen but I wasn't afraid to die.

"This is it," I'd pray, "this is the day I'm going to see Jesus."

I believed Mother Mary would grab me in her arms like she did baby Jesus and take me to heaven. Why did we practice to avoid such ecstasy?

By the time third grade rolled around, I got used to not dying under the desk. Images of children who lived after their exposure to the atomic bombs in Hiroshima and Nagasaki appeared on our small black and white television and I realized there were worse things than death.

Our parochial school teachers taught that the Communists who ruled Russia were going to hell because they prevented Catholics from going to Mass, which the Catholic clergy said was one of the worst things that could ever happen.

As first, second and third graders, my two sisters and I made our own breakfasts and school lunches because my mother's alcohol intake rendered her unconscious in the mornings. We often gathered around her bed trying to figure out if she was alive. *Holy Mary, Mother of God.* One of us would place a finger under her nostrils to feel her breath until, with one exhale, she'd confirm that the worst that could happen, hadn't—and we'd be off to knock on neighbors' doors scrounging rides to school. Throughout my childhood, I had a lot of reasons to think the worst was about to happen every day. But the definition of the-worst-that-could-happen changed frequently, both at home and on TV. Over time these early almost-worst-that-could-happen events immunized me the way a bout of the measles inoculates against future outbreaks. I became fearless.

Eventually we were evicted from our home in Terre Haute (a country ranch house at the foot of an apple orchard). We moved into rooms at the Continental Hotel in Indianapolis. My parents were drinking round-the-clock and couldn't pull it together to find something steady. Which was fine: at eight-years old, I relished hotel living. I learned to run a tab for grilled cheese sandwiches and Coca-Colas in the hotel coffee shop—my parents weren't always available to ask permission. I relied on the hotel bellmen to report my whereabouts when I went out to play in the War Memorial park across the street. The park's gardeners taught me the names of flowers and birds. They never minded the sound of my roller skates as I screeched around the near-empty sidewalks amidst the buzzing bees and trilling birds.

Whenever Agnes dressed for a special occasion, the last thing she'd do is color her nails and lips. She'd sit in an arm chair with high heels dangling from her crossed leg and expertly paint her fingernails using a tiny brush from a little bottle of toxic red lacquer. She never smudged them, never blotched her cuticles, never spilled the polish, never needed to mop up after herself.

First, she'd soak a Kleenex in an upended bottle of Cutex nail polish remover and wipe all her nails clean. The vapors would tickle all the hairs in my nose, and give me a headache, but I never turned away. I'd watch her unscrew the top of Revlon's Fire and Ice and pull out the dark-bristled brush coated in red liquid. With one hand flattened on the antique mahogany side table, and the other one holding the grooved white plastic top, she'd drag the brush along the lip of the bottle to get the exact amount of polish. Pulling the brush from the bottom of the nail to the top in perfect form, nail after nail, she'd quietly finish the job, then blow on the tips of her fingers to dry them. (Where did she learn that? Like me, she was not the kind of person who would have practiced such a thing as a teenager. Unlike her, I've never managed to lay polish or lipstick on myself with such aplomb.)

At the mirror, she'd further glamorize her ensemble with matching lipstick. Gripping a short, thin-handled brush in her right hand, she'd cradle the unopened lipstick in her left hand, slide the top up with her left fingers, and let it drop into the crook where the palm meets the thumb. Holding both parts steady, she'd flick the curved tapered bristles of the lipstick brush back and forth on the creamy substance with her right fingers. Then she'd outline the edges of her top and bottom lips. Next she'd brush the bare flesh inside the lip lines with vertical strokes. With fresh lipstick, her beguiling red lips seemed larger than usual, but not unnatural. (She kept her lipstick and brush in a small leather pouch. Sometimes she left the house with only her Marlboros and her lipstick.)

One day in her room at the Continental Hotel, she painted her nails and lips, slipped into her tweed skirt and cashmere sweater, nylons and high heels and wrapped her shoulders in a mahogany colored mink stole. She had us dress in our Sunday clothes—black velvet dresses and black patent leather Mary Janes. Where were we going? From our rooms in the hotel to the coffee shop on the ground floor behind the French doors off the lobby. It was nothing unusual for my two sisters and I, who'd already learned to sign our names and room number to the checks. But on this day, for reasons I cannot piece together, we dressed for lunch. Perhaps she meant to take us to Mass first. Perhaps she wanted us all to look as if we had been to Mass. Or perhaps my mother had never been in the coffee shop before and didn't know the dress code. She spent most of her time in their hotel room drinking scotch and beer and reading mystery novels. Maybe, oh maybe, she wanted to present a new public face, one of a normal person, a sober, genteel mother with perfect children.

She ordered grilled cheese sandwiches for us all. They were my favorite, but I had begun exploring new freedoms.

"May I please have a grilled ham and cheese instead?"

"Ham? We don't eat ham. What are you, an immigrant?"

Oh no. I folded back into my chair, knowing her mood was about to embarrass me further. Immigrant. It was Agnes' favorite swear word, leftover from the Irish Diaspora when immigrants were tagged as dirty, ignorant, shiftless drunks. Her family had risen above that level. These Tipperary Ryans considered themselves superior in every way—in education, dress and manners. Born three generations after migrant families escaped the Great Potato Famine of the 1840s, they still sneered "immigrant" to separate themselves from their peasant roots, to anglicize their status.

The waitress winked at me as she laid down our sandwiches and Cokes. (We were pals—I waved to her every day when I entered the hotel lobby after school.) Agnes requested mustard. A French's Mustard glass jar appeared on the table. We pulled apart the toasted white bread of our sandwiches and laid them flat in anticipation of spreading the mustard on top of the exposed melted cheese. Shiny yellow cream clung to the insides of the half-full French's. My mother lifted the jar and attempted to unscrew the white metal cap without chipping her freshly Revloned nails. The top didn't budge.

"Goddammit!" she screamed, then threw the jar toward my favorite waitress, who ducked before it smashed against the mirrored wall. "Bring me a jar I can open!"

Not long after, we were evicted from the Continental Hotel.

A Pause to Honor Schoolyard Christs

I don't recall which new school
Girls double dutched on the noon,
Ignoring my scared new-girlness.
Pulled me to them. Here! Like this!
Grab your ends and swing in double time.
Each hand holding a dirty ol' clothesline
Syncopating with the girl at the other end
While one of 'em waited for the perfect time
To lift herself up and jump into the bend.
Then now! my turn to switch my place
Lift up and jump to the slap slap slap
My keds catch, the old rope wraps.
And all the girls laugh with grace
For me who doesn't deserve it
The girl who hasn't earned it.

Chapter 4

We moved to St. Louis. Nothing changed. Eventually we were evicted again, from an apartment building near the Chase Park Plaza Hotel. My father moved us to the suburbs, to Clayton.

For my tenth birthday I bought myself an Elvis pendant at Famous-Barr Company, down the street from our new neighborhood.

I'd never been given money to spend on myself for whatever I wanted before this birthday. Funny thing is, I wasn't an avid Elvis fan. I was a dog-lover. (I scooped up dogs wandering around the neighborhood and penned them in the old empty barn behind our home. I'd feed them, tie them to a clothesline rope, walk them around at night when their owners couldn't see me. After I got caught, there were no real consequences other than I was told to stay out of the barn. I turned my sights on cats, instead. I hadn't yet learned that cats cannot be penned in. I wept every morning when I went to the barn and found the cats had freed themselves.)

To this day I'm not sure what possessed me to use my birthday money on that pendant—maybe I'd heard him singing "Hound Dog" one too many times. I can tell you this, though: I felt triumphant when I showed it off to my mother. And she thought it a waste of money, and called Elvis "white trash." At that sterling instant, I vowed I'd be sympathetic to and defend white trash for the rest of my life. Agnes was an East-coast snob who considered anything west of the New Jersey-Pennsylvania border detestable.

Living in the Midwest was the worst thing that ever happened to her. She called Elvis' Memphis home a "hillbilly hell hole." (Did she know my father's sister and family lived there?). She intended for her daughters to pick up her small-minded prejudices. The other two did. At first I hid from their insults by wearing Elvis in secret.

I was also immersed in a deep friendship with Jesus at the time, and the nuns were constantly reminding me to love God, and love your neighbor. You wouldn't know it from how my family talked about him, but Elvis was our neighbor—as was everyone else in the Midwest. Still, I was not conflicted. Agnes (never "mom"—she and I both preferred Agnes) was wrong. The nuns were right. This burgeoning love for Elvis, my neighbor, soon turned into righteous indignation. After a time, I acquired the power and courage to collect all his records. I played them whenever I could, thumbing my nose at my sisters and mother.

I became an individualistic freewheeling risk-taker—riding my bike outside the neighborhood, wearing mismatched clothes. I changed my handwriting from cursive to backhanded print. When the nuns reprimanded me, I announced I wanted to write like my mother, who changed her own handwriting in high school in defiance of her nuns. I challenged the parish priest and nuns on life and death—still questioning why death was to be avoided, when it meant we'd all get to see Jesus. Some thought I had a brilliant mind and encouraged me. Some questioned my parents about my mental state.

In St. Louis my mother's younger brother Neil and his family lived a normal suburban life on a hill overlooking a kite-flying meadow. After our eviction from Clayton, Neil, whom my mother adored and my father swindled, never spoke to my family again.

Chapter 5

I remember standing in the driveway of our next home, posing with my tennis racket and ball while Gael snapped my picture with our family's 1958 Kodak Brownie. We'd moved to Chicago, to the North Shore, about a month before, and we'd been hitting tennis balls against the garage doors on the west side of the house, a Mock Tudor built into the side of a cliff overlooking Lake Michigan. The sun overhead lobbed burning sunbeams at my squinty-eyed face. Over my shoulder, a fully grown lilac tree emitted a deep purple mid-June fragrance I've never forgotten; the tree drooped over the curvy flagstone stairway leading down to our front door. From somewhere in the upper branches of the evergreens that hugged the short driveway, a robin strung together a complex trill. My mother, not a naturalist in any sense of the word, had somehow known to teach Gael and me to recognize a robin's song, and the scent of lilacs.

We threw our rackets into our bike baskets, squeezed balls into the pockets of our Bermuda shorts, and pedaled down the brick-paved avenue to our tennis lessons at Gillson Park. Gael, a year younger, always aced her lessons, and I always muddled through mine. We were both athletic enough, but Gael outdid me in tennis. I was proud of her, and jealous.

Before heading back home, we rode over to the great ornate Baha'i Temple. It had only been open a few years, but neighborhood rumors said it would soon be closed to the public.

We laid our bikes in the fresh green-blue lawn, climbed the white stairs, and nonchalantly strolled around the outside. All the white doors were open, but we saw no one. The stillness unnerved us. *Holy*. No chairs or pews sat in the white circular sanctuary.

We pulled away from the white marble floor and crept up three flights of white stairs to the white balcony. We peeked into the hush of the white holy. It was a long way down. I held a white tennis ball over the white railing and looked at Gael. Her wide open face said, "Let it go." The ball fell into the white center of the sacred white floor. We froze. No one appeared. Then Gael dropped her tennis ball over the balcony. We crouched down and listened for the echoing plunk-a-plunk, then tore down the stairs and out to our bikes without looking back.

Halfway home we calmed ourselves, exhaled, lost our balance and fell into the lush grass by the side of the road, laughing uncontrollably once more. We quickly got up and pedaled as fast as we could, looking over our shoulders all the way home. Stashing our bikes in the garage as if they were evidence, we kept the secret between us until school started in the fall. Then, feeling invincible, we bragged about the tennis balls in the Temple to our new classmates. Our crime, never exposed to adults-in-charge, fell into an ever-increasing life-bucket labeled "What I Got Away With."

I learned about the geographical heaven and hell in every one of the thirteen parochial schools I attended throughout grade school, including the nugget that heaven was for Catholics only and even that wasn't guaranteed because if I, as a Catholic, committed a mortal sin, I'd go to hell too, or perhaps Purgatory, the halfway house to heaven.

Catholic religious taught me these bits of creep from the official Catholic textbook for children in the United States, the *Baltimore Catechism*, used from 1885 to the late sixties. Even before Pope John Paul II declared in the late nineties that heaven and hell were "primarily eternal states of consciousness more than geographical places of later reward and punishment," Catholic theologians denied that physical Heaven, Hell and Purgatory are part of Church doctrine. But to this day, Catholic diehards hold to the belief that heaven is physically above us and hell is physically below us.

Sitting at the foot of my parents bed one day, I saw a television commercial for the opening of Old Orchard Shopping Center in the next town.

"Where's Skokie?" I asked my mother.

"That's where all the Jews live," she answered.

At eleven years old, I didn't know there were Jews alive in the world. I wanted to ask my mother how Jews were living near us, and not in Jerusalem, like they did when Jesus was around. She detested answering my questions and would have accused me of being an immigrant, a cruelty I couldn't stomach. *Was Skokie hell?*

I always pitied the only non-Catholics I knew—our babysitters—knowing they were headed straight to hell when they died. They'd started watching us soon after we'd moved to the house on the lake. The backyard was shaded by an ancient black walnut surrounded by an over-propagated evergreen garden hemmed with a rusty wire fence. A squeaky gate opened to sand dunes, beachgrass, and a long private beach. My mother hired the seventeen-year old twins to watch my sisters and me on the beach so she wouldn't have to dress for the day and be our lifeguard. And those twins came with boyfriends who had boats. The teenagers taught me to waterski. By the end of the summer my feet were sloshing around in the rubber boots of a single slalom as I skied far out into the lake, unmoored at the edge of the world. I often forgot to let go of the tow rope when we came back to shore for the drop-off. None of them were Catholic and I silently mourned for their souls, asking God why He'd be sending them to hell when they obviously didn't deserve it. After all, they'd shown me heaven.

When winter arrived at the lake I could hardly contain myself. Through my parents' bedroom windows I could see sledders on the hill next door. The only thing separating me from them was a mammoth pile of snow huddled around wild evergreen bushes. All the girls and all the boys, all ages and all sizes, came to slide down Suicide Hill. Firemen hosed it down to turn the soft snow into cold hard ice. Traditional sleds, too dangerous for the slippery terrain, were cast off, piled up in a Flexible Flyer junkyard off to the side. Flat cardboard slabs were the most valuable commodity. We shredded down the hill on the cardboard, sitting down at first, then up on our feet. Eventually we, the first snowboarders, traded cardboard for our boots and slid downhill on our feet.

Girls and boys had equal status on Suicide Hill. There were no rules, no lifeguards, no snowguards, no unofficial self-proclaimed rule-makers. We all raced down the slope, expecting no prize but the chance to bump each other off into snow piles like soccer balls, our unfastened coats flapping in the wind even as winter reddened our noses and our bodies grew warm with fever. Medics and parents came to bandage limbs and scrapes. Ambulances carted broken bones off to Evanston Hospital. Exhaust smoke obscured our vision of cars double-parked on the street where parents arrived to yell: *Let's Go!*

And when the stars came out we gathered down the street at No Mans Land for hot chocolate, competitors no more. We belonged together, heaven or hell.

On May 30, 1957, Zengeler Cleaners in Winnetka phoned my mother to congratulate her for winning a portable black and white television. It was a contest I'd secretly entered on her behalf when we were running errands together. Agnes was on her way out the door to Evanston Hospital to have a baby, but she glared at me—I had made a grave error in writing down her name and phone number and throwing it in the fish bowl. We were not allowed to let strangers into our lives through the telephone.

Colicky Stacy came home a few days later, shortly after the surprise TV. Our 38-year-old mother, weakened by anemia and alcoholism, went to bed for three months, and delegated the care and feeding of the infant to my sisters and I. Ten-year-old Gael spent endless steamy hours sterilizing glass baby bottles. We all took turns feeding the baby. Twelve-year-old Maere used her authority as the oldest to redo the assignments in order to do the least amount of work. Meanwhile our father was commuting to downtown Chicago by train from our anglicized Irish-American enclave, as part of a brief effort to be a sober citizen, husband and father.

She had many names before she was Stacy. For months we simply called her The Baby. My father suggested Stacy. My sisters and I, having never heard the name, loved it, as if it were a name for a cat or a dog. Agnes liked the name because of the intrigue attached—it's a nickname for Anastasia. (In 1957, Anastasia, the daughter of Tsar Nicholas II, was rumored to be alive and living in an adopted family. Treasure hunters searched for her endlessly even though all evidence indicated that the Bolsheviks killed her and her family in 1918.) Agnes' penchant for strange names seemed to be borne out of a desire to be as unmotherly as possible. (Her favorite fictional character, Auntie Mame mocked convention and social mores, drank a lot, and collected bohemian friends.)

Stacy was born at the beginning of summer, and Agnes insisted I walk her around our neighborhood in her baby carriage, hoping the shadows and sounds would soothe her distress. Agnes' constant reminder stays with me, "Be sure you stop under the trees for the baby to see the shadows."

"Women should always have babies in the beginning of summer," she'd say. "In case they're colicky, they'll be soothed by leaves swaying in the trees." She muttered *immigrant* (maybe *idiot*) under her breath anytime another mother announced the birth of a baby in any month other than summer. And indeed, three of her four babies were born in May, June and July. She pretended she planned it that way.

Agnes was right about how nature tranquilizes infants, but she never claimed it worked for adults. She wouldn't have been caught dead using such an unsophisticated, sappy remedy herself. Her tranquilizers were beer, scotch, and valium.

Carl Jung tells us Agnes simply passed on an inheritance—the collective unconscious of Irish tree worship that supposes tree fairies live in high branches watching over us. My mother's life was rooted in addiction—less like the tranquil trees, and more like the life-sucking aphids. Yet, her words gave my family a love for trees—a priceless, ancient, tranquilizing inheritance.

When she was out of diapers, I rode Stacy around on my bicycle bars, introducing her to the birds, the sky and clouds. I had a hunch that her life would be happier if she could name her birds before she had to memorize the ABCs. Meanwhile we were evicted, from the house in Wilmette, and from another in Kenilworth.

We moved to rural Lake Forest, where I regularly rode Stacy the few miles to the Burns family farm. The ten-child Burns family had a barn with a pool table, ping pong table, pinball machines, and a refrigerator full of Cokes; a field for tag, football, and baseball; a stable full of horses. I played with the older Burnses, Stacy played with the younger.

One day panic shot through all the play groups when we realized Stacy was missing. She liked to wander off to the stables; our biggest fear was that she'd been trampled by one of the horses.

The police came. She was nowhere on the property. As the day came to a close, a strangulating fear hovered near. But finally a policeman pulled into the driveway with Stacy in the front seat. He found her walking a half mile down the tree-lined country road. She was simply going home.

I came to the T-junction, missed the stop sign, and was driving headlong toward the ditch before my father's well-restrained voiced boomed, "Whoa! What are you doing?"

I slammed on the brakes and muttered the best apology I could manage as a twelve-year-old: "Oops! I forgot I was driving."

"That might be a problem in the future," he wise-cracked as he motioned me to back up onto Ridge Road for the drive home.

Earlier that night we'd been to the Lake Forest Cinema for Agatha Christie's 1957 courtroom drama, *Witness for the Prosecution*. As the soundtrack began in the near-empty theater, my father had said, "I'll give you fifty cents if you guess who did it within the first five minutes." Midweek movie-going with my father wasn't uncommon, but it happened sporadically. This spontaneous outing hadn't given me any time to consult with my movie-savvy friends, and at twelve, I was not yet habitually reading reviews in the local paper. My father usually summarized the plot in the station wagon on the way there. But not this night. It was a mystery.

"He did it," I'd whispered to my father at the five-minute deadline, guessing that the accused murderer played by Tyrone Power had, in fact, committed the murder. It was nothing more than a risky whim.

He'd rewarded me with not only the fifty cents, but my first driving lesson. So I had good reason for missing the stop sign. My mind was consumed with its own cleverness, and my spirit was somewhere in the cosmos, idling on my father's approval.

A nun once told me a father's approval is a gift from God— she said this, presumably, to keep me on the straight and narrow. Driving my father around that summer fused my blind loyalty to both. We drove after dark to avoid getting caught by the police. My mother was privy and pleased, but we didn't tell my three sisters. I was developing a taste for secrets and lawlessness.

Eventually I bragged to Gael, and she begged me to teach her to drive.

She sat in the driver's seat while I stood outside, wedged between the body of the car and the open door so I could point out the particulars on the dashboard. She stretched to reach the pedals, and all of a sudden the car lurched backward, slamming me against its side before banging to a halt at the fence. I was badly bruised, and Gael's kitten got crushed under a wheel. She was hysterical, but I wasn't concerned about her, the kitten, or my own injuries. I felt only a freon fear of my father's disapproval.

In the fall, at the suggestion of a college classmate named Charlie Camalier, my father took his active alcoholism to Mexico City on a business trip. He planned to raise money from the Buckleys, an old-money American-Mexican family who were friends of Charlie. His scheme was to use the Buckley money for a venture to sell and barge Indiana coal down the Mississippi, across the Gulf of Mexico to South America. He left my mother, my three sisters and I in a rented, modern, low-slung rural house. We had enough money to pay the bills through Thanksgiving. But my father's drinking drove him into the arms of one of the Buckley women, who kept him lubricated and entertained and cycling between Mexico City and Cuernavaca well into the spring.

As our household money became scarce, my mother came up with a solution: teaching me to shoplift. As we crossed the threshold of the local grocery store on Waukegan Road she gave me my first instructions: "Do what I tell you in here, don't question me, keep your mouth shut." We moved casually through the aisles as she piled up cereal, milk, and bread in my crossed arms. At the meat case she magically transferred all the goods from my arms to hers while grabbing a big package of ground beef, slipping it into my wool coat and whispering the next instructions. "Button up." Sliding into the busy check-out with me at her side, she plunked down her groceries, paying the bill on the least expensive items while I hid the meat in my coat. In a flash we were out the door, in the car and driving safely home. This new side of my mother's craftiness created within me a kind of wild admiration; I was thrilled to be in her secret cloak-and-dagger world.

In December the telephone company cut our service for non-payment; the operator announced it to anyone who called our number. My mother resorted to using the outdoor pay phone at the train station on Route 41 to try to get ahold of my father. She developed bursitis in her left shoulder that winter, and I'd often do the driving, then sit in the heated car watching her shake in the freezing cold, icy tears numbing her cheeks while she cried obscenities to whomever was on the other end of the line.

Here and there, I dutifully rode my bicycle the two miles to the grocery store, guided by my mother's secret backdoor instructions. I accepted my introduction to the criminal underworld without question, never even wondering what would happen if I got caught shoplifting. God had entrusted me with this grave responsibility, and I knew He would insulate me from any ensuing consequences.

Occasionally a glorious snowstorm illumined my bike ride, whereupon my piety would kick me into high gear: "This is nothing compared to what the martyrs did. I love you Jesus. Give me courage, strength and joy." I was an eighth-grade Catholic school girl who loved the saints and dreamed of becoming a nun. But Jesus was not my only source of strength. I was spurred on by the unspoken secret admiration of my mother. She seemed proud to have produced and trained a family hero. We bonded as equals that winter—secrets between us alone. I knew her and she knew me, and she could count on me, her favorite.

The entire east side of our one-story modern wooden house had floor-to-ceiling windows. Heating the place through that upper-Midwest winter cost more money than we ever had, so we relied on the living room fireplace. Firewood was plentiful—I pilfered it from the neighbors' woodpiles after I finished my homework, stealing during the late news so I could return in time to watch *The Tonight Show* with her.

I had acquired a job feeding two black Labrador Retrievers; they belonged to neighbors who lived on the other side of the woods. The dogs lived in an outdoor pen attached to an indoor heated shed with a small kitchen where I prepared their specialized dinners. I rarely had to face the owners—they even left my pay in the dog shed. Their woodpile, neat as a new box of crayons, had a woodchuck burrowed inside. I didn't worry about leaving traces of my thievery when I grabbed their logs because the little fellow, my accomplice, disturbed the snow around the pile. Screwtape-like guilt—that is, the gradual, gentle kind of guilt—eventually convinced me that they, and all the other neighbors, knew I was the cause of their dwindling woodpiles. I averted my eyes and dodged their greetings whenever I saw them passing me on the road or in the grocery store.

Every once in a while my father managed to wire enough money from Mexico to the Lake Forest Western Union office for us to get the heat back on, the telephone ringing again, and gas in the car; we could take honest outings to the grocery store. My bicycle then was restored to its rightful place of honor, no longer a tool with purpose, but the seat in which I was one with God.

The infusion of money seemed like God's way of protecting me from being exposed for my sins. It saved my mother from ever having to awkwardly pretend she was shocked and ashamed by my marauding and shoplifting—which she never had to do, because I never got caught.

That was the winter of my twelfth year—the year I learned to love my mother.

A Pause to Address Mary Reilly

Ridge Road was for modest vehicles, for landowners and families, deliverymen, trash collectors, handymen, maids, sheep and that's it, because the country road rolling along the distant end of our North Shore suburb past big old generational homes like yours, the one modern one (mine), and the one sheep farm, it was a quiet one, disinviting disturbances, while inside *Meet the Press* murmured on Sunday mornings before Mass and the nightly news narrated the evenings before dinner, but you, Mary Reilly, clomped five miles down Ridge Road on your horse and brought another for me to trail-blaze in the sheep fields and eat wild raspberries in season then ride through the back brush to your barn spying on your mysterious brothers and their polo ponies, making the best of memories in a time that held the worst for me inside my family's rented mid-century modern that reeked of cigarettes, scotch and Budweiser—outside, chlorine rose from the pool my mother cleaned for us, that we swam in after horseback riding in the summer—then in the fall Sacred Heart Academy took us in navy blue blazers for French and Religion, The Mikado and recess and lunch with the nuns and Cuban girls from the revolution; after school I avoided the shame of the empty ice box and food cabinets and met you on Ridge Road to ride our bikes with my baby sister on the handle bars past the sheep farm to the Burns family compound for softball and ping pong, joking around and drinking Cokes in the Burns family kitchen watching horses in the fields and chickens in the coop, a respite from my house down the road where talking was dangerous and lies took over and my father was absent for long stretches, commuting to the city and flying to Mexico on extended business trips, and my mother drank all day and night and I wondered if she was still alive in the morning because she didn't wake to wrap peanut butter and jelly sandwiches in wax paper and boil soft eggs. (What about yours? She had something wrong with her, did she drink too? Was she sick?) Then learning to drive on the macadam driveway in the white station wagon when my little sister Gael ran over her kitten, *splat!* hysterics all around except me—I went numb, wise to parents not giving a damn behind the flat walnut door to the Mies-like architecture where danger lurked and drunks stumbled but where, once, pointing out the bathroom window at eye-level with a tree limb, my mother showed me a robin's nest holding blue eggs, and when I told you, you said, my father told me your phone is disconnected because you didn't pay the bill, and *Boom!* that was the end of our friendship, right there at the lunch table in front of the muchachas who didn't speak English and the Cuban girls who did and the French nuns *Mon Dieu!* alarmed but inept when it came to reprimanding you, you double-crossing rat bastard— whatever happened to you?

Chapter 6

The Academy of Sacred Heart, where I started eighth grade, was my twelfth elementary school. It had a reputation for encouraging rivalry—rewarding grades at an all-school weekly assembly where medals and cross-body ribbons were ceremonially bestowed on the girls.

From the start I intended to excel in all subjects, especially my nemesis, arithmetic—no matter what was happening at home. I was not going to disappoint myself or my parents. I'd make this the final school of my elementary school life.

Sacred Heart was more rigorous than the previous school, Faith, Hope and Charity in Winnetka; I crammed my head with Latin conjugations, algorithms, periodic tables, *Romeo and Juliet*, diagrammed sentences, the French Revolution, and the Gospel of Mark. At the end of the year the Mater Admirabilis Award (Mother Most Admired, another name for Mary), an Oscar-like trophy, would be bestowed on one student for her excellence in academics, sports, religious and civic activities. Her name would be engraved on a bronze plate and permanently fixed next to the previous winners. I prayed every day for God to keep me in that school through the end of eighth grade so I could win that prize. I tricked myself into believing that if I worked hard enough, I'd remain, somehow, in one place.

The nuns, formally known as the Society of the Sacred Heart, and informally known as the Madams, had been in Chicago since 1858, when Bishop Anthony O'Regan brought them from France to open a school at Rush and Illinois. They trained women to be leaders in society as well as teaching simple social graces and homemaking skills as was the custom at the time. The nuns moved the school to pastoral Lake Forest when hotels, saloons and brothels flooded the Rush Street neighborhood in the early nineteen hundreds.

Fifty years later, French expressions still permeated Sacred Heart's routine activities. *Congé* (holiday) was a surprise day when schoolwork was replaced without notice by a day of fun such as playing *Cache Cache*, a version of hide-and-seek. Congé ended with *Goiter* (to taste), a roomful of refreshments to celebrate the winners of the day's games. This *joie de vivre*, coupled with the nuns' love of God, appealed to my awakening soul.

My teachers gradually increased my extra credit assignments to include tutoring the younger girls, writing for the school newspaper, public speaking, acting and sports. As the end of the year approached, my classmates started congratulating me, knowing my name would be forever on display in the trophy cabinet. I was in the number.

In the school bus on the way home from an ordinary day in early May, I thanked God for Sacred Heart and my soon-to-be immortality. Then the bus driver pulled into our driveway and slammed on the brakes. Furniture, clothes, pots and pans, bicycles—everything we owned—clogged the pavement.

I told my sisters to stay on the bus, until I saw my mother sitting on the couch with three-year-old Stacy. I ran out to save her from a reality I didn't understand. There was no sign of my father. He was still in Mexico. A sheriff blocked us from entering our house.

Agnes' father, Granddaddy, wired emergency money from New Jersey to save his daughter and four granddaughters from homelessness. We fled to downtown Chicago into a suite of rooms in the Pick-Congress Hotel across from Grant Park. Us girls all slept in one room, Agnes in another. Warm lake breezes floated through the open windows over our untucked sweaty bodies at night. While my sisters slept, I sat up in bed and laid my head atop crossed arms on a windowsill. I gazed into the interior courtyard.

The hotel's atrium was like a big hole in the middle of the building. The roof of the one-story lobby on the first floor connected the secret stories of the travelers, honeymooners and evictees collected in the rooms above. Everyone's windows were open. Lights were out. White filmy curtains lay still between my eyes and strangers' nightlife. Sounds from other rooms peaked and lulled. A woman sang the same bars over and over from Marvin & Johnny's doo-wop, "Cherry Pie."

I knew little of sexual love. Once upon a time, my naked mother woke me in the night, commanding, "Don't you tell your father!" as she hid in my closet. His naked body found her anyway. He dragged her by the hair down the hall and slammed the bedroom door behind them. She cried out and I knew I couldn't save her. The screams stopped—an abrupt deadening silence. Sure that she had died, I hid under my bed in case he decided to come for me.

The next morning I tiptoed to the bathroom, grabbed a towel and wrapped it around their bedroom door handle. I wanted to soften any sound as I turned it to sliver open the door. My mother's chest heaved softly, a sign I recognized as life. So I joined my sisters in the kitchen to fix my dish of Cheerios and watch cartoons. When my parents appeared, she had a black eye. No one talked.

I imagined the Cherry-Pie singer languishing in a red silk slip with her groom in ways I'd seen on television shows: stroking his hair, kissing his cheeks with her crimson lips between drags on her cigarette. He'd ask her to serenade him with *Cherry Pie. Cherry, cherry pie.*

In the few days we lived in the Pick-Congress, I never saw my father. I did see his clothes and shoes strewn across the roof of the hotel lobby though, as I was peering down into the atrium. He must have returned from Mexico, found our whereabouts, and shown up at my mother's room. Visual evidence of their rage-fuelled arguments was rare. Usually the chaos and destruction stayed on the inside.

But Agnes had finally had enough. (I did, too, but I had no way out.) Two weeks later I was living with my mother's relatives in another school, in another town, another state.

Chapter 7

I hear some people say they knew this or that at age five, six, seven or eight. They knew there was no Santa Claus, or that their father was having an affair with the neighbor. Not me. Throughout grade school, with all evidence to the contrary, I trusted that the adults in my life knew what they were doing, didn't lie to me, and moved our family around for good reasons, like better neighborhoods, or better schools. Then my mother yanked us from our midwestern roots, away from my absentee father and to the East Coast.

My sister Gael and I landed at the doorstep of my mother's sister, Aunt Joanne, in southern Maryland, with her husband Bill Dorsey and their seven children. It was the beginning of May and we entered St. Mary of the Assumption School, where the nuns "sought to imitate Jesus Christ." The school was segregated except on the playground; there I joined girls and boys, blacks and whites, all defiantly playing baseball altogether.

The eighth grade class at St. Mary's had spent the entire year before I got there memorizing one poem a month. In order to graduate, I had to memorize all nine poems. Not only did I rebel against this arbitrary standard, I became hysterical over it. My mother had taken two of my sisters to New Jersey to live with other family members, and for the first time in my life I absolutely knew that she had gotten it wrong. I needed her with me, to defend me against the injustice of those nuns. I had sacrificed a lot for her, and it was time she helped me.

Uncle Bill had a different idea. He told me I could do it, that we'd do it together.

Never before had anyone sat me down and given me a pep talk. Every night after dinner for six weeks he helped me learn those lines. Poems like *Annabel Lee* by Edgar Allan Poe, *The Tyger* by William Blake, *O Captain! My Captain!* by Walt Whitman and my all-time favorite, *The Chambered Nautilus* by Oliver Wendell Holmes. Uncle Bill's love flowed through me and poured out onto the paper, lighting up the poetry. He gave those words to me. And now, when I hear or see them, my heart pounds with a thunder of love for his eternal soul.

The Dorseys threw a party on my thirteenth birthday, right before graduation. They invited all their friends and children. My mother arrived with my baby sister. The backyard ballooned with streamers and bunting, barbecue, birthday cake, and something I'd never seen before—a keg of beer. Uncle Bill gave me the first draw of the tap. I gulped down the Budweiser without tasting it. My first beer. Then I had another. And another. I suddenly became someone else, united to those around me. I belonged—in that family, at that party, with those saints. I was in that number.

The St. Mary nuns weren't very good at imitating Jesus. But Uncle Bill? He was the real deal.

Stacy was four that summer when my mother moved us all to the Jersey Shore. My sisters and I took turns watching her at the Atlantic Ocean, which was a few blocks from the home Grandaddy had rented for us. On Labor Day weekend the beach was packed with our new friends and all our cousins. Large cliques sat around on top of beach towels, smoking cigarettes, gossiping, reading movie magazines, and playing cards. The blue-sky day hosted a wild ocean, foreshadowing a hurricane coming up from Florida. Swimmers dove under the swells out to the stillpoint, the spot on the ridge of swell to catch a wave and ride headfirst all the way into the pebbly shore. Hyper-vigilant lifeguards kept an eye on every person who entered the sea.

Each of my sisters and I expected the other to be watching Stacy. And she went missing. The entire beach turned itself over hunting for her. I panicked, knowing we were in big trouble for losing her, no matter what happened next.

A cousin found her looking up into the trees walking down a shady sidewalk away from the beach. Once again, she was simply going home.

When Irish immigrants came across the sea, they carried their old-sod superstitions with them, hidden in the crevices of their narrow minds. Displaced men and women of the Famine learned quickly to silence these myths in an effort to assimilate into nineteenth century anti-Irish America. For instance, in Ireland mothers would never coo over a baby or express its cuteness, for fear of lurking turncoats overhearing the compliment and stealing the baby to sell to the Brits. Similarly, parents didn't praise their children, lest the mythical faeries replace them with the faeries' own inferior little people. The Irish knew the truth of it because their fair babies were a much sought-after treasure. The threat of stolen babies was real.

This probably explains my parents' deep-rooted resolution to give only puff-praise to their four daughters, as in "your hair looks nice" or "I like that dress."

When outsiders would tell me "your parents must be proud of you," at making the high school Honor Roll, or induction into the National Honor Society, my response coiled up in my throat, strangled in self-loathing. I never heard them say anything like "Good job, we're proud of you." I doubt they knew about faerie child abduction; these superstitions disappeared from consciousness within a generation. (And if they did, they'd never have admitted it. They both abhorred Irish peasantry.) But never-praise-the-children was in their DNA. They couldn't help themselves. I yearn for their approval still, long after they've died.

When I entered my first non-Catholic school for freshman year, Agnes wouldn't allow me to enroll in the necessary-for-the-rest-of-your-life typing course. She even tried to block the school from requiring me to take Home Economics; she thought it was degrading to be taught to clean your home. These confusing embarrassments were as close as she ever got to hinting she thought I may have qualities that would lead to a higher calling—which, to her, was anything other than wife and mother. She told me if I knew how to type, my husband would use me as his secretary, and if I learned to clean house, he wouldn't pay for a housekeeper.

Ironing, though was a different story. She taught me to iron. Agnes went to church at the ironing board. It relieved her hangovers, and calmed her nerves. In every house we moved into she found a sanctuary for ironing—a laundry room, spare bedroom, basement.

No, Agnes did not iron for a household of four children, so we could have ironed sheets and pillowcases, or freshly pressed school uniforms. Her ironing was reserved for her alone. She laid out her Oxford cloth shirts or linen dresses on the ironing board, placed a dampened dish towel over the garment, and pressed down with a hot iron until steam rose up; then she'd move to another spot, re-dampening the towel when it dried out. Her eyes winced at the clean hot steam. The acrid smell of damp cotton or wool flared her nostrils. As she conquered the wrinkles at hand, her malcontented brow smoothed out. (Her sister Joanne, after a few bourbons, would often eulogize her with, "Your mother loved to iron.")

★

After she left my father, Agnes made valiant efforts to sit her four daughters down to dinner every night. We never ate before eight o'clock, unless we were at someone else's house. She deemed it ignoble to eat before the early evening news was over. Most of her recipes, clipped from *The New York Times*, required long simmering or baking times to suit her cocktail hour, which often lasted until nine o'clock. I didn't mind eating late, because I rode my bike around town with the neighborhood boys after their dinners and before mine. I did my homework while watching the late news and *The Tonight Show* with her.

Agnes' beef stew was extravagant. She would not permit anyone to call it Irish stew because, "Everyone knows the Irish have lousy taste and can't cook." Neither would she admit that it was her version of the *Times'* recipe for *Boeuf Bourguignon*. Her process would begin with a cast iron frying pan for searing the two-inch cubed sirloin pieces in hot bacon fat. She'd remove the meat and clean the frying pan to sauté the sliced onions, mushrooms and carrots in butter. The two most important ingredients, the hard-to-find dried bay laurel leaves and the bottle of red wine, were added to the meat and vegetables along with salt, pepper, thyme, allspice and garlic cloves. All of this simmered in the Revere Ware stock pot while Agnes sat in her favorite spot on the couch with her scotch Old Fashioned to watch the news.

Around seven o'clock, when the saucy aroma started permeating the house, she'd stir the pot, turn off the stove, and return to the living room for an extended cocktail hour with her boyfriend and whatever teenage boys had stopped in with their illegal six-packs to gossip about the neighbors. Agnes told her own funny stories, and the boys all thought she was hilarious. About half-past eight she'd skim the fat off the ragout, heat it up, add thickener and a few more ounces of wine, and we'd all sit down to dinner.

I can't remember how old I was when Agnes started cooking with wine. It became fashionable in the fifties long before Julia Child's TV cooking show—probably after the war. I overheard Agnes extolling the virtues of cooking with wine "rather than cheap cooking sherry" on long-distance telephone conversations with her sisters as they swapped recipes. She added wine to marinate and gravy, chili con carne, shrimp Newburgh, beef stroganoff, spaghetti sauce and anything else she could get away with. If she invited one of the drop-in cocktail guests to join us for dinner, she'd add more wine to the dish to expand the quantity. As we got older, she cooked with more wine, less water. Once in a while we'd get a guest who was unfamiliar with Agnes' version of gourmet dining. But otherwise, no one complained.

In the early sixties, a new boy arrived at the Jersey Shore from California. He brought a skateboard. Someone made other ones for my friends and I using old roller skates and plywood. We skateboarded downhill in forbidden cemeteries until dark, or until the local cops chased us away. Skateboards were outlawed by adults, not because they were dangerous, but because they were unknown, noisy, not a part of the mainstream, and therefore somehow subversive. We hid them in car trunks and behind old tires in the garage. None of us had standard-issue parents, so we formed our own family. For a time that family stuck together, laughed a lot, and listened to each other's woes and dreams. We vowed to call each other, not our parents, if we ended up in the police station for trespassing in our various skateboarding haunts. Later on, one did, with a bale of marijuana. He didn't call. He went to prison. Another drank too many beers, drove himself into a tree and died.

Todd Sterling, a frequent guest and favorite of my mother's had had a crush on my sister Gael ever since we moved into the house down the street. They dated in eighth grade, but she lost interest, and he and I became inseparable friends for one important summer.

The two of us sat in slatted wooden seats on the aisle halfway back from the stage in the Asbury Park Convention Hall at our first concert. The Hall's open doors and windows allowed the smooth ocean breeze to float in and around to cool us. It was 1961 and we thought we were the only Joan Baez fans on the entire Jersey Shore. The overflow crowd stunned us.

Until then, our only experience at a live performance was the Manasquan High School variety show. We lived in the remains of the fifties' cultural wasteland, where the middle class would never spend time or money on concert-going. Ignorant of concert etiquette, we refrained from singing aloud but mouthed all the words as our folk hero transported us—"All My Trials," "House of the Rising Sun," "10,000 Miles". Before intermission Joan Baez introduced her friend from Greenwich Village, Bob Dylan. *Oh no! I had saved my babysitting money to see Joan Baez, not some unknown.* Onto the stage came a scruffy little curly topped blue-jeaned boy who played guitar and sang a solo, "Freight Train Blues." They sang "Man of Constant Sorrow" and "Pretty Peggy-O" together. Even though Todd's favorite singer was the Godfather of Soul, James Brown, he shared my instant joy and devotion to the twangy-voiced Bob Dylan. Dylan and Baez sang their love for the poetry of those old folk songs. And we shared a love for the singers with strangers from our own land.

We started reading *A Coney Island of the Mind* by Lawrence Ferlinghetti, and we'd write beat poetry in the hangout we created in my mother's garage. There was an old couch and a rickety TV table for our record player. We listened to music and drank beer undisturbed during the day when everyone else was at the beach. My mother accepted my summertime retreat; she never used the garage and was happy to be removed from the sounds of folk music, Motown and Elvis. She seemed to like some music, Keely Smith and Louis Prima, but she had no interest ever in buying or playing records, or even listening to music on the radio.

Todd and I saved money from our part-time jobs to buy 45 rpm records. He caddied at the local golf course. My waitressing job in the coffee shop on the Asbury Park boardwalk gave me more money than I'd ever thought possible. But the job didn't last long. I had trouble turning away from the seagulls fighting over dead fish on the beach long enough to write "pancakes and bacon" on my order pad. And I wasn't overly attentive to the old guy telling a story over and over about the 1934 wreck of the SS Morro Castle on that same beach. The manager suggested I look for another job when I dropped a gallon jar of syrup on the floor in front of the swinging kitchen doors.

One day my mother found us in the garage with empty beer bottles, practicing the Twist and the Mashed Potato. "Degenerates!" she exclaimed. "Go to the beach!" We ignored her, roiled with laughter and gloried at being characterized as degenerate—an anthem of the beat generation. For that one summer, we were officially beatniks.

The chilly weather and start of the new school year gradually closed the garage door. Todd's studies took up his time. And I sought other hideaways where I could drink beer all day, listen to music and flirt with boys.

"Only niggers drink gin in the winter," Agnes said when I came home drunk one afternoon after school. As if there was no possible grounds for dispute. As if there was a difference in what I drank when I was only fooling around with my friends, having fun, looking at boys, and trying to feel something I read about in the brochure in the drugstore. (Her words seemed off-putting then, abhorrent now.) The Northeast winter had its grey, bone-chill beer, scotch and wine. But why no gin? When I repeated this dictate later to one of the boys, he said "She's so white." It took a lot of gin in the winter for me to finally get that.

The Jersey boys didn't exactly line up at my door. Unless they were looking for my sisters. All that changed around my fifteenth birthday when I started drinking gin. Throughout one hot summer a Jersey boy tuned his car radio to WINS at the drive-in and we settled into the backseat of his 1958 baby blue Chevrolet Impala convertible with a bottle of Gilbey's.

The first time I'd laid eyes on him, he was dancing with his girlfriend at the Friday night high school canteen. They danced in perfect syncopation—the Twist to Chubby Checker, the Mashed Potato to James Brown, and the Stroll to "Sea of Love." They were like American Bandstand stars. By the time I turned sixteen, he was out of high school and working as a mailman. When this sandy-haired tall-bodied man asked me out, he smoothed out my insecurities. A cool handsome guy seemed attracted to me. We saw each other a lot, and even though he had no other girlfriend, I don't ever remember thinking of him as my boyfriend.

Each of us must have had an unspoken pact about why we were together. I know we talked about "Sea of Love" as if it were our song. Whenever it came on the radio we'd assemble ourselves, and get out of the car, and he'd dance me around the way he did when he was a star at canteen, except we had to hold each other up.

I learned a lot from him. Seeing him mopping up the remnants of my over-ginning all over the inside of his Chevy told me men would do anything for love.

Soon my body was no longer able to handle the sustained adrenaline rush from loving boys. I hungered only for the peace I found in gin. When I lay naked and hungover with yet another Jersey boy in the basement of his family's beach bungalow, I was able to keep up with giggling talk of marrying and concocting funny names for our children, but I was bored by the ho-humness of conversations about maintenance love. When that boy returned to school in Philadelphia I went to another. I was drowning in a sea of love.

In late summer of 1963, I ran away from home: away from my mother, away from my three sisters, from the Jersey boys and our year-round Jersey Shore house. I loved the five-block bike ride to the Atlantic Ocean, but not even the beloved beach could keep me near my mother's unpredictable, screeching, violent rampages. Agnes' alcoholism was in full force; she had no idea how to parent her teenage girls, especially with me in my own early stage of alcohol addiction.

I fled to my father, two hours away in Manhattan. He'd moved there to be close to us and to try, once again, to stay sober. My mother had suspended her hatred of him long enough to allow a few visits between us, but when he'd moved into a new girlfriend's suite in the Delmonico Hotel on Park Avenue, my mother had cut off all communication.

He checked me into my own hotel room, across the hall from the suite he shared with his girlfriend. I enrolled in the Junior class at Marymount School of New York, a Catholic girls' high school on Fifth Avenue; there I became fast friends with a classmate whose father managed the Waldorf-Astoria. I was, of course, no stranger to hotel living. The shame I'd felt as an eight-year old living in an Indianapolis hotel (instead of a house like other families) had melted away; in early 1960s Manhattan I put on a full-blown girl-of-privilege sham that took years to shed. On an obsessive quest to meet Bob Dylan, I slipped in and out of Greenwich Village coffee houses, lying about the folk singers I'd met. I secretly flew to Boston on the fifteen-dollar shuttle for overnight stays with a Boston University undergrad I'd met in a bar over the summer, returning in the morning with sweaty, debilitating hangovers.

In early December at the Delmonico, I woke to a fiery, closed throat, and a vice-grip headache. I went by ambulance to the emergency room of New York Presbyterian Hospital and was diagnosed with mononucleosis, hepatitis, and migraine. The doctor explained that mononucleosis is called the kissing disease because it's transmitted by mouth. *Oh shit.* Shame ran in my veins alongside the incapacitating virus. I was afraid everyone would find out I was kissing a lot of boys and having sex.

Treatment included nausea-inducing morphine injections. To heal my inflamed liver I laid flat on my back for thirty days— through the Christmas holiday. Classmates from Marymount brought homework; friends from the Jersey Shore snuck in beer; my boyfriend flew in from Boston with a stuffed Wile E. Coyote; a cousin sent a case of Reese's Peanut Butter Cups.

While I was in the hospital my father rented a furnished three-bedroom apartment overlooking the Wollman Skating Rink in Central Park. Prolonged bedrest in the new home helped me recover. The compulsory homework necessary for me to move on to my senior year slipped from my hands and onto the floor as I slept off my diseases. I returned to school after four months and failed that year with a humiliating final average grade of 34.

Chapter 8

John F. Kennedy was still alive the September I drove with my father in his white Cadillac Eldorado down the pike from our new home in Washington to the boarding school in Virginia. My head overflowed with questions. Will they have a television? What will I do after school? How will I wash my clothes? I dared not ask my father, for fear he'd mock my questions. In his silence I could hear him say, "They're nuns. They take care of people. Stop worrying." I wasn't worrying, simply wondering. In spoken language between us, different words seemed to have the same meaning— wonder and worry, driving and speeding, drinking and drunk.

Unfamiliar signs became our talking points.

"Oh, there's Fredericksburg. Didn't something historic happen there?"

"It's a Civil War town. Ten thousand slaves ran away from the plantations and joined the Union Army."

Slaves? I had never been in a place where slaves had lived.

"Monticello. Is that Jefferson's home?"

Petersburg.

Appomattox.

I'm not sure how much I knew of Civil War history or American history back then, heading towards another junior year in high school, but clearly the road signs along the Virginia highways had awakened some schooling. My immature view of life misinformed me. I thought the places I read about in history books, like these, no longer existed.

Until then, I had lived my whole life at sea level—the flatlands of the Midwest, at northeastern Illinois' Lake Michigan and the New Jersey seashore. The Virginia road climbed up and down; blue and green wavelengths, tree-lined hills with wide verdant medians. My mother used to call me a nature lover, and I guess she was right: the scenery captivated me, as if we were driving through the Garden of Eden. I imagined Paradise at the end of our journey.

What's the Blue Ridge Parkway?

My father had already been on Skyline Drive, the main road through Shenandoah National Park on the Blue Ridge Parkway. He reminisced about his time at Massanutten Military Academy before he entered college. It had given him a lifelong hatred of the military.

At Richmond we turned southeast toward the Norfolk Naval Base, Hampton Roads and Williamsburg. It didn't feel like I was leaving anyone behind. My mother, sisters, cousins, friends and lovers were living in another place, another time: wild summers and grey winters. Meanwhile my dissolute life had brought me here, to Walsingham Academy, a school for girls from mothers who didn't mother and fathers who didn't father—girls who had ulcers, girls who dyed their hair.

We turned onto Jamestown Road toward my new post. Fear tightened.

Had he told the Mother Superior I had mononucleosis?

Got drunk?

Swore?

Didn't believe in God?

Had had an ectopic pregnancy?

Did he even know I was tired all the time, and lost?

I feared and I hoped they'd care for my soul.

The academy, established in 1947 for the local Catholic children, provided a boarding school—mostly for quasi-orphaned adolescents from military and foreign service families. My roommate, a school veteran from Washington, gave me the low-down on all the other boarders and the nuns.

"This is the place parents send their daughters when they don't want them anymore," she said.

I do not remember my response.

"It's named after the Our Lady of Walsingham in England. Mary appeared there in 1021," she went on.

"Really?"

"Yes, and they believe it."

On my first off-campus unchaperoned outing with fellow castaways, I led the coquettes to a local bar in the center of Williamsburg for a raucous afternoon of drinking with the local boys. We returned to campus vomiting and spitting obscenities. The nuns pegged me as the ringleader and cloistered me until after Christmas vacation. Initially I spent Saturday afternoons laying on the floor with a legally blind classmate listening to books on long-playing vinyl records sent to her by the Library of Congress. Thomas Wolfe's *Look Homeward Angel* and *You Can't Go Home Again* were her favorites, and we heard them in their entirety—a few times. I folded in on myself, doomed to moping around the boarders' quarters listening to depressing literature, daydreaming, and sneaking cigarettes.

On Friday afternoon, November 22, 1963, I walked through the empty school cafeteria to pick up the receiver hanging from the pay phone in the corner. As I said hello, I noticed the cooks in the back of the kitchen huddled around a radio. Agnes was on the line.

"Are you all right?"

When I was fourteen-years old, I had immersed myself in the 1960 presidential race. Agnes hardly listened to me when I talked to her about it—what adult listens to a fourteen-year-old?—but when it came time to vote, she asked me what to do. She didn't want to vote for a Catholic. Now she had to report that my hero and our former neighbor, President John F. Kennedy, had been shot. She was visiting her old friend Ted, and suggested I catch the bus from Williamsburg to Washington to join them. I was under no one's legal custody, but my father had given the boarding school nuns orders prohibiting me from seeing my mother. I frantically called my father and asked if he'd sign off on letting me go to her. He said no.

I slinked over to sit with the downtrodden cooks as they listened for any morsel of hope. There was none. We lamented together—me and these black kitchen workers from southern Virginia, slave descendants whose hope for civil rights laid in the Kennedy White House. My sorrow could never touch the depth of theirs. They comforted me, as if my heritage had also been clouded by the despair of violence. They made me theirs. I was in the company of saints.

The nuns moved us boarding students back and forth to chapel throughout the weekend. They allowed us to fill the rest of our hours watching the assassination drama on TV. The next week I visited my father over Thanksgiving weekend. While he and I were sifting through the magazine rack in People's Drug Store at DuPont Circle, the store radio blurted out President Lyndon Johnson's proclamation that Florida's Cape Canaveral would now be known as Cape Kennedy. (Ten years later Floridians changed it back.)

"Hear that? Never forget where you were when you heard that," he said.

Washington sputtered that weekend in the aftermath of the assassination and the funeral—no one moved except the crowds advancing to JFK's gravesite at Arlington National Cemetery. At seventeen and without a driver's license, I capitalized on my father's somber distraction to hone my driving skills with his car, visiting school friends who were home for the holiday. Everyone was glued to their TVs, trying to settle their own emotions. I escaped the collective mourning, red-lighted my feelings, and spent time alone learning to navigate Rock Creek Parkway, the notoriously confusing Pierre L'Enfant circles, Key Bridge, Pennsylvania Avenue and the cobbled streets of Georgetown. I stayed in the Northwest part of the city, sensing something sinister about Southwest, Southeast, and Northeast Washington.

I cruised by the home I'd occupied with my parents and two sisters a dozen years before, wondering what had happened to our family.

Back at school, still suffering through my lonely punishment, I despaired. Sister Walter Mary heard my silent *cri de coeur* and rescued me from my Saturday afternoon dirges. She had me study articles from the *New York Times*, and a new Catholic literary magazine, *Ramparts*. Within six months of its beginning, *Ramparts* morphed into a hotbed of radical political thinking. Thomas Merton, Howard Zinn and Eldridge Cleaver wrote for *Ramparts*. We discussed the articles, and she guided my thinking into concrete opinions. I wrote letters to the editor which she edited, typed, and mailed in my name. Did she know she was radicalizing me? I loved the reading, writing and, most of all, discussions with Sister Walter Mary. Before Christmas she engaged me as her silent partner and taught me to edit the school yearbook and newspaper.

After Christmas vacation I would have been free to go to town with the other girls who continued—despite the threat of reprisal—to meet boys, smoke cigarettes, and drink beer. But before my first Saturday outing I was punished for smoking in the laundry room and—you guessed it—campused again for the rest of the year. My bittersweet confinement put me back in the crosshairs of my kind and dedicated teacher.

In the spring, Sister Walter Mary took us to the local mental institution, Eastern State Hospital, to prepare the Catholic children for their First Holy Communion. Yes, children. I have no idea why there were young children locked up in an insane asylum, but I was shown how to teach these pre-Ritalin six-, seven-, and eight-year-olds to memorize answers to such preposterous questions as "Why did God make me?" from the Baltimore Catechism. In preparation for this duty, a hospital attendant gave us tutors a ground-floor primer on insanity—pointing out those who were paranoid-schizophrenics, psychopaths, and catatonics as we walked through the wards and saw the caged young children. Some of the children sprang at the chain-link fences like Spiderman, spitting and yelling obscenities. Others rocked on their haunches chanting incomprehensible words. And one sat perfectly still with a fixed stare. The tour guide said she was catatonic, and assured us we would not be teaching this group of children.

Still, all in all it was a kind, comfortable atmosphere. The hospital—the oldest psychiatric facility in the country—had been founded on the concept of "moral therapy," with organized exercise and social activities incorporated into treatment. ("Moral" in the sense that insanity was treated as an emotional disorder, not a wanton behavioral condition.) I ended up tutoring a little girl who wanted only to play with my hair. I'm not sure how much she learned, but I got to help her dress up in her white veil and gloves and participate in her First Holy Communion ceremony with the local children at nearby St. Bede's Catholic Church.

Back at school, in her efforts to keep me out of trouble, Sister Walter Mary volunteered me to tutor the sixth graders in the day school for their Confirmation lessons—more memorizing from the Baltimore Catechism.

Walsingham held a student-led Democrat-Republican combined mock convention. It was 1964, and I was assigned to be Nelson Rockefeller's campaign manager. I wrote to Rockefeller's campaign office in New York explaining I needed Rockefeller's platform in order to make a speech at our mock convention. I received crates full of campaign buttons, posters, leaflets, scarves, ties, cufflinks, bracelets, position papers, and even a suggested stump speech. I plastered the school with Rockefeller posters and made sure every student had some sort of paraphernalia with "Nelson" on it.

I was already accustomed to debating politics. When I was a freshman, I knew a boy who always spouted anti-government diatribes from the John Birch Society's *Blue Book*. I had to read it to refute his claims that Communists had infiltrated the civil rights movement, labor unions, and the Democratic Party. I have no idea where I got my liberal views as a young teenager, but I eagerly engaged in defending civil rights against the tyranny of the privileged white class, my friends. But now I had been assigned to the other side, at least for the time being. I debated in the hallway, at the lunch table, in the girls' room—anywhere I could engage students.

Organizing the students to chant "Nelson! Nelson!" at the mock convention, and then delivering the nominating speech—these things electrified me. My candidate won the student endorsement by a wide margin. This was my first taste of political action, and I'd learned valuable lessons: winning elections was all about talking up the candidate, and giving out a lot of stuff.

All the Seniors were required to enter an annual statewide Virginia Catholic Diocese Writing Competition. The topic for my year was "vocations," and I thought I'd have a chance at winning if I stood out from the crowd. My well-researched theme held that nuns should take a non-teaching sabbatical during menopause, because the consequences of their changing hormones made them ineffective educators. I submitted my essay "The Menace of Menopausal Nuns" to Sister Walter Mary at the deadline, the Monday before Thanksgiving.

Expressing my opinions required a kind of prudence I hadn't yet learned.

On Tuesday, I was suddenly summoned to the Mother Superior's office. My packed luggage was brought to me, and I was taken to the bus station. Expelled. No warning. No goodbyes.

It didn't help that my father had declined to pay the school tuition that semester.

I never saw Sister Walter Mary again. I hope she knows I read *Ramparts* magazine until it folded in the seventies, and that I still write letters to the editor of any old publication I feel like.

My father, trapped in the throes of a months-long binge, had invited a fellow active alcoholic to live in our apartment in Washington. When I arrived, their round-the-clock drinking left no time, and no place, for me. She had taken over my room and thrown all my belongings in the dumpster. I overnighted in a hotel, cried myself to sleep, and took a bus the next day to my mother's house in New Jersey.

Chapter 9

Quelle difficulté! Conditional and subjunctive tenses, reflexive verbs and object pronouns—back at Manasquan High School for my senior year, I'd missed too much time in French IV class, and I knew, I *knew*, that I was doomed to fail. The week before graduation, I crept into the last make-up session to take a stab at the French IV final. Monsieur reached into his *attaché* and, without regard, handed me the test. At my desk I read "Final Examination French II." This *coup de grâce* ignited my innards. "*Bon chance*," I imagined him saying, "my gift." I had failed most of my senior year classes; he surely knew an A on the French final was my only chance to graduate. Was the French II exam his *détente*? He'd given me an A on the same exam in sophomore year, when I was still an *ingénue*. Unable to face the powerful truth— that he'd made a *faux pas* in giving me the wrong test—I handed him the completed pages, averted my eyes, and scurried out the door. Having spent most of senior year in the parking lot with my beer-drinking *clique*, I was a cheating teenage *cliché*.

(When I first met Monsieur, way back in my freshman year in French I, I'd innocently pretended to be a *savant* until he realized I'd studied French in grade school. He guided me to advanced classes and nominated me for the National Honor Society. He was a serious teacher. In the spring of sophomore year I'd joined an *esprit de corps* that joked around, got drunk, and swapped stories about sneaking out for a secret *rendezvous*. Monsieur had warned me about drinking and boys. And sure enough, within the year I was in the hospital with mononucleosis, worried about unwanted pregnancies.)

Now, in the days before graduation, he confronted me in the hallway about the final exam mix-up. I was confounded at how to engage in a mature *tête-à-tête*. The fear of not graduating after spending five years in three different high schools paralyzed me; I feigned ignorance.

"So," he said. "We are at an *impasse*."

That impasse—trying to forge ahead while living under a cloud of guilt and shame—would stalk me through graduation, college, *beaucoup* jobs, two marriages, motherhood, and the regeneration of my dry bones.

I was born into an imaginary bohemia—that fabled *café* society populated by French-speaking hard-drinking *avant-garde* artists, unconventional writers, intellectuals and *dilettantes*. My mother had probably sensed it at the cord-cutting, when she'd decided to name me Regan. This literary baptism into the world of King Lear conferred on me the subliminal message that fathers, representative of all men, are bullies. My parents were a unique throwback to the Lost Generation—well-dressed gypsies who didn't pay their bills, lied, and cheated, but still had cocktails and *hors d'oeuvres* every night before dinner.

I moved into my bohemian mind around fourteen after reading Sartre's *No Exit*, fruitlessly peppering adults with questions like "Do you believe in God?" and "Do you think hell is other people?" Why did I think people talked about these things in *bourgeoisie* mid-century America?

One Christmas in late adolescence I found myself feeling out of place while guzzling Budweiser at a family party. I weaved over to my grandfather, who had been a sailor in Word War I.

"I've been reading *The Naked and the Dead*." I said.

"What's that?" he barked, annoyed that all of a sudden he got stuck with one of his idiotic teenage grandchildren.

"*Naked and the Dead*, you know, the Norman Mailer war novel." I said.

"So what?" my grandfather snapped.

"I was wondering if you felt dehumanized when you were in the Navy." I said.

"It was the best time of my life," the inebriated patriot sang.

"Well," I asked, "were you afraid you were going to die?"

"Of course not! I was on the finest ship in the Navy—indestructible."

"Was it lonely?" I asked.

"What the hell kind of question is that?" he shouted. "You don't get lonely on a ship full of men. They were the best friends a man could have. What are you trying to prove, anyway?"

"Oh no! That did it! Now he'll be talking about the war all night." Aunt Jean said over her shoulder, "Look what you've done."

"For God's sake, Jean, she's trying to make conversation," my mother came to my rescue.

"It's the wrong conversation for this house," Jean-the-hostess said.

"The war? Since when are we forbidden to talk about war?" Jean's husband weighed in.

"Not war, dear, the first war." Jean said. "We only talk about the Second World War now."

"Since when?" he shouted. "I don't want to talk about that war!"

"That's because you spent the war drunk in the Brooklyn Navy Yard being pampered by your mother who took you to dinner every night in Manhattan," Jean shouted back.

Grandaddy had set himself up as the paterfamilias of my East-coast family. He was the last of thirteen children born to Irish Catholic immigrants who'd come from a sparsely populated settlement near Cashel in Tipperary. As a child I'd constantly heard the fantastic tale of how St. Patrick had driven the snakes out of Ireland on the Rock of Cashel, plus the more important (and equally fictitious) story of how he'd converted all the pagans to Roman Catholicism. This fallacious folklore also exalted the Ryans to an undeserved status, as if they were the first Catholics in Ireland. Unearthly powers infused the Ryan family DNA, marking Grandaddy the irrefutable authority on everything.

Grandaddy was providing our living expenses; he'd forced us to move from the vestal suburbs of Chicago to the concupiscent Jersey Shore. Under no circumstances would Grandaddy pay for us to live in the Midwest, a region of the country he considered inferior. He and my father were both alumni of Georgetown University Law School and were constantly sparring to see who was the slyest fox in the room. My father knew he faced arrest for non-payment of child support if he ever set foot in Monmouth County; Grandaddy had filed a suit against him on behalf of my mother.

When my older sister graduated from high school, she dimwittedly invited my father, whom she believed would fund her college education. My father daringly appeared at the threshold of Maere's outdoor graduation ceremony, and Grandaddy signaled to the Sheriff standing by to handcuff him and haul him off to the county jail. Subsequently it became apparent that my mother manipulated Maere into setting up this debacle; it had all happened at Granddaddy's dictate.

To avoid thinking about my father's confinement in the nearby county jail, I turned ever more to rock 'n' roll, alcohol, and the company of boys. My grandfather wanted my sisters and I to testify against my father at the trial, holding our living expenses over our heads. Eventually my father outfoxed Grandaddy, got out of jail, and fled the state. He never did pay alimony or child support.

Chapter 10

Waiting for the 10:20 at the sleepy Sea Girt train station, I re-examined my ensemble. My navy blue linen skirt and freshly ironed pink cotton blouse self-wrinkled in the morning August sun. *Damn. I'll look crumpled by the end of the train ride.* I extended my lightly tanned, clean-shaven leg, black flats. *Should I have worn nylons?* I worried.

The train whistle tooted out of the nearby pine trees south of the station. I waved at my mother stopped in her car at the flashing gate. *All abo-aarrd*, the conductor crooned to me alone. No other passengers boarded the mid-week run. Comforting old cigarette smoke seeped from the upholstered seats in my train car.

My bamboo-handled Bermuda purse held a five dollar round-trip ticket, bus fare to the unfamiliar Manhattan address that was my final destination, and a French copy of Albert Camus', *The Stranger*, which I decided to read as penance for cheating on my French final. I cracked open the book and cursed myself for forgetting a pen to underline and make notes. I tossed it aside.

The Jersey Coast Line stops at twenty-three towns before reaching Penn Station in Midtown Manhattan. At some stops—Belmar, Asbury Park, Avon, Long Branch—I daydreamed of recent hoopla in local bars, on beaches and boardwalks where I'd spent my teenage summers. I had to force my mind back to my mission—asking my father for the five-hundred-dollar tuition I'd need for college.

I must rehearse, I kept saying to myself. *Let's see, I'll get there about one thirty. If he's getting up from the night before, a simple approach is best.* I knew he'd want to get rid of me right away. So: *Hello Daddy, I need some money.*

Then again, if he was binge-drinking, I'd need to acclimate him to a conversation, repeating myself several times: *Hello, Daddy. I have a partial scholarship to college. I had three jobs this summer but still don't have enough money for the rest. It's five hundred dollars. Yes, yes. I got a scholarship. No, it covers only fifty per cent of the tuition. Yes, I got a scholarship. No, it's only half.*

At Penn Station I still didn't have the right words. My stomach churned on the bus. He opened the door to the borrowed apartment in a blue terrycloth robe and demanded to know what I wanted. Empty bottles of scotch and ashtrays full of Camel stubs filled every surface. Sweat trickled down my legs. I never sat down. He found his checkbook.

"What's the date?"

"August 6, 1965."

He threw the check at me. I risked examining it for the amount, date and signature.

He raged, "You don't trust me? Get out of here!"

I delivered the check to the financial aid office at Monmouth College in Long Branch and asked them to cash it immediately.

Three days later Maere answered the telephone at home. With undisguised glee and *schadenfreude,* she relayed a message from the college: my father had stopped payment on the check. She acted as if this were proof I didn't deserve to go.

In the weeks that followed I scrounged up a scholarship and entered my Freshman year. I made it through three semesters.

Chapter 11

Jim Murphy and I met on the back of a Honda 250 Dream when he gave me a lift home one night in the early summer of 1966. We'd been working underage at a bar in Avon-by-the-Sea; we'd traded glances but not names. Our mutual attraction accelerated on that motorcycle, on raucous dance floors, and in the soft sand under the boardwalk. He was a junior at Princeton; come fall, I was motoring an hour west every weekend to party with him.

By December, I was pregnant. I thought I should have an abortion. He said I had to decide on my own. If I kept the baby we'd marry. If not, he'd never be able to see me again. How could a twenty-year-old college student know that? He had more confidence than I, and seemed less emotional. We shared a love for beer, the beach, and rock & roll. But it wasn't a partnership. I was alone.

She wasn't hard to find, this illegal woman in Newark. When you reached a certain age in the sixties, everybody knew someone who knew someone. I drove alone, climbed the wooden stairs to the three-story house, and knocked on the rattling screen door. She answered and asked my name. Nothing came out of my mouth. She suggested I come back when I'm ready, but "don't wait too long."

Instead I drove to Murphy and we started a family.

★

I dropped out of college. We rented a two-bedroom above Toto's Market on Witherspoon Street. Murphy studied Sociology and had a coveted job driving around campus picking up and delivering student laundry. Everybody knew him.

Our baby boy, Joe, was born in May of 1967. I babysat for professors at night while Murphy studied at home and bonded with our son.

The baby fit perfectly in his plaid vinyl car bed on the backseat of our 1954 Plymouth. But his father thought his growing body would be more comfortable on the floor in front of the passenger seat of a sports car. When fall classes began we traded the four-door sedan for a body-scarred 1959 spruce green Austin Healy ragtop. The four-seater sported a long hood, a trunk the size of a bicycle basket, and not enough room in the back for an infant in a baby carrier. Joe gurgled happily riding around Princeton on the floor.

As a new mother, I applied Dr. Benjamin Spock's child-rearing ideas—to treat children like individuals, to be flexible and affectionate—to week-old smiles, chronic cries in the night, and cross-the-room sprints when he learned to locomote at only nine months old. Dr. Spock's instructions emboldened me to stand my ground in the whirlwind advice from mothers, aunts and grandmothers. I learned to ride the baby on the back of my bicycle, and to animate the world; I pointed to clouds, trees and cars as if I'd never seen these things before in my life.

Cars and motorcycles were distinctive then—make, model, year—and Murphy loved them all. His family never tired of ridiculing him for buying a broken motorcycle when he was fourteen, taking it apart, and then failing to reassemble it. (He sold it in pieces in a wooden Florida orange crate.)

★

One weekend in March, Murphy decided to head down to Florida with my mother's boyfriend Harry for the annual Sebring twelve-hour race, the U.S. equivalent of France's LeMans Grand Prix. Baby Joe and I stayed in New Jersey to help rev up the 1968 presidential campaign of poet-senator Eugene McCarthy. We roared down the highway to Trenton in the gas-guzzling Austin Healy. There, I hoisted Joe into an Army surplus knapsack (with cut-outs for his little legs), and joined McCarthy-for-President volunteers to knock on doors before the primary.

On the way home, whipping down Route 1, the entire ragtop blew off and got chewed up in the tires of a tractor trailer. The rumbling of the engine through the floorboard must have acted like a sleeping machine for Joe. He stayed conked out for the rest of the trip.

I phoned Murphy in Sebring, fearing a full verbal throttling about the cost of a new roof. But he just laughed: "Just turn up the heat!"

Murphy and I both supported Eugene McCarthy, the peace candidate, not only because he vowed to end the Vietnam war, but because he announced that one of the first actions he'd take was to fire J. Edgar Hoover. Hoover, a symbol to us of everything wrong in America, reportedly had secret files he used to blackmail politicians into complying with his agenda. We applauded McCarthy's courage, and figured he was indeed "Clean Gene"— that Hoover had nothing on him. Robert Kennedy entered the race after McCarthy nearly beat President Johnson in the New Hampshire primary in March. This turned up the heat on the McCarthy volunteers, and Joe and I spent a lot of time on that highway in the topless car driving to and from Trenton.

Friends from the Jersey Shore weekended with us whenever there were house parties at Princeton's off-campus private clubs. Most were young women looking for smart rich bachelors. The class of 1968 was the first with more public- than private-school graduates. Murphy belonged to Cannon Club, whose members were primarily public school scholarship students. They called him Madman. Broken jaws, concussions, and sutured lips were as commonplace as t-shirts and blue jeans. Everyone would huddle around the bottomless keg of Budweiser in the basement, rocking out to *Mustang Sally*. Every year they'd mourn the loss of a Cannon Club member who'd died in a drunken car crash.

Beer was the primary social lubricant at Cannon Club. The scholarship men fearfully adhered to Princeton's strict anti-drug policy. The campus prohibition against alcohol was not enforced. The ban on women in the all-male sleeping quarters was enforced, but before we moved in together Murphy lived in Rockefeller Suites, which was unofficially off-limits to campus police. Everyone in the suite had a compact fridge crammed with bottles of Budweiser.

While Madman Murphy was completing his undergraduate degree, the campus firecracked with information sessions on avoiding the draft, small anti-war rallies, and civil rights demonstrations. A month before graduation Martin Luther King, Jr., was murdered. Riots broke out in Trenton, halting my campaign activities. Classes were cancelled the day of his funeral, and an overflow crowd filled Alexander Hall for his memorial. I joined campus conversations that tried to set an agenda to carry on Dr. King's non-violent vision.

As the wife of an undergraduate I had very little expendable income, mostly from my babysitting money. I saved for months to pay a local seamstress to make a gown for the most momentous social bash of my life—the 1968 Princeton University graduation ball. The Simplicity pattern for a trumpet dress formed an a-line chemise with angel-wing sleeves. The dressmaker lengthened the trumpet hem to conform to ball-gown fashion. As I described it to my mother over the phone, she carped that it sounded like a hippie dress.

The Chinese red background of the silky fabric set off overlapping geometric shapes in primary colors—blue rectangles, green squares, yellow stars and purple crescents. No, it was not a hippie dress. It was psychedelic. I'd wear pearls at the circular neckline to prove I was more than equal to the socialite dates of the Ivy League graduates.

On graduation weekend, Madman and I intended to keep a lid on our drinking, but once we broke into our case of beer the morning of the ball, we threw away the lid. The national torment about Vietnam, the heartache of Robert Kennedy's assassination the week before: we had plenty of excuses.

My temperate in-laws arrived to mind their grandson and celebrate with their son. I gloried in my avant-garde, trendsetting gown, but at the ball I felt a certain boozy inferiority when I fidgeted for my pearls and realized I'd forgotten them. Without my pearls I was a lesser presence, not a part of the party.

The next morning I awoke at Cannon Club in the loft reserved for out-of-town dates. My eyes opened to half-digested food and liquor splayed across my custom-made dress. I stumbled home barefoot, and as I reached the top stair to our apartment the waft of a normal morning hit me—bacon, eggs, toast, coffee. My revitalized, exuberant husband and his always-forgiving parents were gathered around the table, feeding the baby and readying themselves for the graduation ceremony.

I avoided their gaze, excused myself to the bathroom, threw my scarred dress in the corner, got in the shower, and prayed for redemption.

The early summer foliage that June morning barely shielded the unsympathetic sun as I walked with my in-laws and the baby to the outdoor graduation on the Nassau Hall lawn. My hangover emotions betrayed me as I wept through the class president's recap of the chaotic year. To top off the violent stew that led us to mistrust our leaders, draft deferments for graduate students had been revoked the week before. I stared at a sea of men who had no idea how to plan their futures. Madman Murphy barely escaped the draft. We married the last year marriage was allowed as a deferment.

Afterward, I hurried home and tossed the pukey gown in the trash, determined never to be reminded of the hours I lost at that graduation ball.

A sensible car replaced the topless Austin Healey. Meanwhile our marriage was running out of gas. Though we loved each other, we couldn't power through the next-day sorrow of deceptions and disappointments.

Murphy graduated and we partied through the summer at the Shore. While he lifeguarded, one-year old Joe and I romped on the beach. We delighted being together in the light of day.

At night, Murphy and I took turns going to bars with our friends. I started smoking pot and instigating arguments about the looming Democratic Convention in Chicago. Jersey Shore barflies had nothing on me—I'd been schooled by Princeton peace activists and *Ramparts* Magazine.

President Lyndon Johnson did not seek reelection. That left Eugene McCarthy, the intellectual standard bearer of peace and justice, to shepherd the frenzied world toward utopia. He won the New Jersey primary in June and I felt redeemed, as if my work for McCarthy offset my dismal behavior. I was nine days short of the voting age of twenty-one and couldn't even vote for McCarthy in the primary, but I had high hopes for him in November.

I tutored a young cousin and used the money to buy stationery and postage stamps; I joined a letter-writing campaign to Bobby Kennedy's old delegates. We asked them to vote for McCarthy at the Democratic Convention in August. I'd pontificate to friends and strangers on the beach and in the bars to test out new reasons to support McCarthy over the late-arriving establishment candidate, Vice President Hubert Humphrey. I fully expected my work to pay off at the convention in Chicago, and I longed to be at the youth festival planned in my erstwhile hometown to celebrate Clean Gene's victory. By the time I joined friends at a neighborhood saloon to watch the convention on TV, news accounts of the protests and riots were interrupting coverage of the political speeches inside the International Amphitheatre. But that didn't matter to me. Soon all would be well. McCarthy would clinch the nomination and beat Richard Nixon in November. No doubt about it.

The unthinkable startled me out of my innocent political bliss. The TV flashed back and forth between old white men bullying peace delegates inside, and police beating peace activists outside. Mayor Daley ordered the police to shoot to kill. People who looked like me were dripping in blood.

What was happening? Eighty percent of primary voters were anti-war. We won the battle and I was sure we'd beaten back the war machine. But the delegates rejected McCarthy and his peace plank, nominated Hubert Humphrey, and iced out Democratic activists.

And me? I added daily drinking, LSD, mescaline, amphetamines, Librium, and cocaine to my diet. I could see no future.

Murphy applied for a job at the Atomic Energy Commission, an anathema to the peace movement, and although he wasn't hired, we argued about it endlessly—the ridiculousness of an ideologically in-sync couple fighting ferociously over too fine a point.

Murphy decided we'd go to Michigan State in the fall, so he could study for a graduate degree in Sociology. I loved his resolve, his yearning to serve the needs of others, and his commitment to Joe and me. But my interior life was a scrambled mess of self-doubt and shaken beliefs. I craved marijuana.

Richard Nixon beat Hubert Humphrey in November. The first vote I ever cast was for Hubert Humphrey for president. He lost by 1% of the popular vote and 110 electoral votes.

"Do you believe in God?" I asked Murphy as he studied.

His answer didn't matter, I simply wanted him to talk to me. He didn't. He couldn't. I busied myself with babysitting and mothers' groups, riding Joe around Michigan State on the back of my bicycle, attending any free lectures and movies I could find. Joe and I marched with the national anti-war organization Another Mother for Peace. We demanded a boycott of cereal companies that advertised during violent cartoons on Saturday morning. An expose about a Michigan State University group that worked in Vietnam as a front for the CIA sparked protests in front of the University President's house. I wrote endless letters to Congress demanding an end to the draft. But mostly I wrote long letters to my friends agonizing over being trapped in Spartan Village, Michigan State's married student housing. I really craved pot.

Late in the spring, I packed up Joe and flew home to the Jersey Shore to stay with my mother. Neither of us thought we had a problem, and we drank together all the time.

When Murphy returned from Michigan, we moved our family into a rent-free eight-bedroom mansion overlooking the Atlantic Ocean. He spent the summer evenings and weekends painting the exterior clapboard. When he came home from his day job as a mailman, I was usually gathered with an assortment of friends on the massive outdoor porch, drinking and smoking pot. We often made tie-dyed t-shirts in one section of the kitchen while someone cooked in another. A thieving butcher joined the growing band of revelers. I, well-practiced in the art of larceny, would descend on the A&P and buy steaks and ribs that he'd stickered with a $1.29 price tag. The cannabis-hungry party washed down the end of the mournful sixties with Rolling Rock and Boone's Farm Apple Wine while barbecuing cheaply procured bone-in ribeye steaks.

There were friends returning from Vietnam, psychologically scarred and addicted. An AWOL Navy guy read books on schizophrenia all day. We role-played encounters he might have with a psychiatrist so he could mimic insanity to get out of the war. The MPs eventually caught up with him; the last I heard, he lived in the psych ward in the Brooklyn Naval Hospital, by then truly deranged.

Drinking and pot-smoking reached a tipping point somewhere in the haze of that summer. Marriage mystified me. Why was I expected to cook dinner every damn night? Madman and I yelled at each other all the time. I took toddler Joe with me to my mother's, then a series of friends. I hoped Murphy would come for me. When he did, I was too stoned to see him.

I thought I stepped up my drug and alcohol use because my marriage fell apart, or because Richard Nixon was President, or because King and Kennedy were murdered, or because John Lennon married Yoko, or because my father abandoned me—any reason other than the truth: I simply couldn't stop once I started.

Father Long—my mother's cousin— spent a few weeks every year near Sea Girt. That year, he asked to meet on the wrap-around porch of a worn-out nineteenth-century hotel on the Atlantic Ocean. Assuming he wanted to force feed me unwanted marriage counseling, I hung an anti-establishment roach clip on a leather string around my twenty-two-year old neck to amplify my defiant hippie ensemble.

He talked about my marijuana use. "Give it up. For your mother's sake."

"Are you talking to her about her giving up drinking? For my sake?"

He'd once worked as the disciplinarian of an inner-city Catholic boys school. Realizing I was no match, I made a fast exit. As I scrambled out of the painted-wood rocking chair, I heard him shout over my shoulder: "I'll pray for you."

His summer vacation had been interrupted by my mother's cry for help—help for me, her addict. Agnes never even mentioned the word "pray," to say nothing of actually directing her thoughts towards the prayer realm. How drunk must she have been to ask for help from her cousin, a soldier of God?

Murphy dropped by my friend's place on Thursday afternoon, August 14, 1969, to fetch Joe for the weekend. I lay in bed with my sister's boyfriend smoking pot next to the crib while the two-year old napped. The three of us had a grand argument. Murphy grabbed our little boy, screamed I would never see either of them again, and bolted from sight.

The next morning, I hopped in a station wagon with my sister, the boyfriend, and a few merry-making hippie wannabes; we were headed for three days of peace and music in Woodstock, New York. The car roof was overloaded with tents, sleeping bags and cases of Rolling Rock. We squeezed a change of clothes, toiletries, and festival tickets into our Army surplus backpacks, along with plenty of hallucinogens.

Turning off the New York state highway onto the country road leading to Bethel, we fell in line with a flotilla of vehicles— three lanes undulating up the two-lane road. We shared joints and beer with new friends, and danced alongside cars to the tunes blaring from their radios. After a few hours we pulled into a roadside clearing and set up camp with other squatters.

Afraid someone would pickpocket our tickets, we concealed them as we set out on the twenty-minute march to the festival. We came up over a rise to the clear acoustic sound of a song we'd never heard, but were bound to never forget: "Freedom." There were no ticket takers, no souvenir stands, no fences, no security guards. All of life gently moved downhill toward the music; we plopped down on a perfect spot with Richie Havens in sight.

Wavy Gravy announced to the crowd—500,000 people—that we shouldn't eat the brown acid, and that there was free food in the Hog Farm tent. A lone helicopter whirled in and out of a landing spot near the stage. Cardboard crates full of donated ice cream sandwiches, oranges, and apples were unloaded and then passed overhead to the hungry throngs.

Paranoia struck. Someone said they were Army helicopters. A rumor spread that the government had gathered all the hippies in one place to drop bombs on us. My friends trickled back to the cars. I remained. Rain fell sometime in the night, and again the next day. I crawled under a stranger's tarp, sleeping off and on, waking for Santana, Canned Heat, The Grateful Dead, Creedence Clearwater Revival, and eventually the Texas twang of my hero, Janis Joplin. *Take another little piece of my heart!* Finally Sly and the Family Stone rocked the muddy land as I wandered through the thinning crowd.

Early Monday morning I found myself among a group of tattooed bikers. I thought I should be afraid, but they shared their drugs, food, and drink. We were at perfect peace as Jimi Hendrix came to the stage with his band, Gypsy Sun & Rainbows, nine hours later than scheduled. He lifted us all into the fifth dimension with his crazy electrified Star Spangled Banner. We claimed Hendrix's version for our ourselves—it was our own national anthem, because we loved America, too.

★

The party was over. I stood alone on a sodden, garbage-strewn hill. A friend appeared who had stranded his car on the festival road. We laughed and cried, moseying along with other stragglers who were searching for their rides.

Squinting through the sunny day, we drove down New Jersey's Garden State Parkway, finally landing in the sobering net of the state police. I gulped down our stash of opium to save us all from legal harm.

Coming home from heaven, I faced the consequences. I vowed to clean up my act—so so happy I hadn't made that vow before the weekend. I retrieved Joe after a sobering conversation with Murphy and his parents. I promised to change.

Chapter 12

That autumn I got word the Vietnam Moratorium Committee was planning what would be the largest antiwar protest in United States history.

I set about convincing our drinking group at McCann's Tavern in Belmar to drive the four hours to the March on Washington. Even though everyone simply wanted to drink and have a few laughs, I kept it up.

"Forty-five thousand American troops died in the past two years. If we don't end the war your draft deferments will be revoked. Wanna get drafted?"

That did it.

Two carloads of us drove off after last call. Since I'd lived in Washington as a teenager for a few months with my father, I drove the lead car, pretending I knew the directions.

When we arrived, yellow school buses were pulling up bumper-to-bumper around the White House in order to block President Nixon's view of the protesters. We headed to a friend's place near DuPont Circle to sober up and eat. Reeking of coffee and cigarettes, our speed-freak friend had been up all night working in a restaurant, but he hitched on to our party and created an all-out breakfast banquet. They all fell asleep. I dropped a diet pill and took off for the Lincoln Memorial.

Peter, Paul and Mary and Arlo Guthrie belted out tunes between speeches from anti-war Senators Eugene McCarthy and

George McGovern. Peace hero Dr. Benjamin Spock, whose book had taught me how to be an engaged mother, told us half-million idealists that we were all noble. *I was noble.* Pete Seeger led the crowd in the singing of John Lennon's "Give Peace a Chance." I have loved sing-alongs ever since.

Back at the crash pad I hustled my friends outside to join the protesters marching toward DuPont Circle. We all got tear-gassed, screamed for mercy, helped each other to our cars, and tore out of town.

(When the war ended, six years later, none of them had been drafted.)

I drove to Vermont with Tricia and our children in her Ford Falcon to escape our husbands, and our debauched lives. It was just in time for the fall color. We rented a four-bedroom apartment on the ground floor of an old Victorian farmhouse on the village green in Pittsfield. Three-year old Joe slept on a top bunk, and Tricia's two-year-old and nine-month-old slept in bottom bunks. Four other separate apartments sheltered hippies, ski bums, drop-outs, draft dodgers, divorcees, dharma bums, dogs, cats, and a runaway Playboy Bunny. We worked the snow season ten miles up the road at bars, restaurants, ski lifts, and resorts on Killington Mountain, the East coast's largest ski resort.

Exchanging job information with our new neighbors joined us one to another. Friendships accelerated and deepened on pot-and-wine-induced astral planes. Our apartment housed the only permanent children, but there were plenty of visiting kids. Whenever a neighbor started planning a communal dinner, the buzz hearkened merrymakers to come down from the mountain and join in a mind-blowing meal.

The California hippies made their own yogurt. We all ate it plain. The East-Coast hippies knew the location of every New

England health food store where we could find unsulfured raisins and whole wheat bread. Some were schooled in unique nutrition practices and taught us new ways to cook and eat. Steam your vegetables. Throw raw sunflower seeds in your salad. Eat lots of brown rice. Don't eat meat, except for bacon.

The favorite dish, Mishmash, was a twenty-four-hour affair. The beans soaked in apple cider vinegar overnight to release the scum that causes digestive problems. Then the rinsed beans simmered for four hours with mashed garlic cloves. Early arrivers pitched in to chop fresh tomatoes, green peppers, red peppers, red onions, zucchini, yellow squash, mushrooms and celery. Boone's Farm Apple wine and a few tokes of marijuana usually sufficed to keep the cooks focused on their tasks, and free from worldly concerns. The fragmented vegetables eventually landed willy-nilly into crackling olive oil in a magnificent skillet, a paella pan we'd found in the Rutland rummage shop. Meanwhile the washed brown rice seethed unstirred in its own pot for an hour or so. Some lucky soul folded the cool beans and hot rice into the simmering vegetables. At this point, someone usually scooped some into a bowl for the children. Then the dominant chef in this communitarian gaggle would stir in a dollop of honey, fresh-ground pepper, fresh basil, chopped jalapeños, paprika, grated ginger, and crushed marijuana. The Mishmash settled on low heat it emitted a blended fragrance evocative of Old Mexico. The aroma told us when to eat.

More cool cats usually appeared at the dinner hour, whereupon someone would add extra marijuana to the Mishmash. The California hippies served up yogurt to top off the stew. Some diners carried full plates to gatherings in other apartments. Most of us sat here and there, relishing the sweet and savory peace of our groovy family.

Tricia and I drew closer through our love for beer, pot and men. New Jersey friends up for ski weekends, and co-workers from the resorts, all flocked to our door for after-hours revelry.

We relished breaking the chains of constraint that had kept us from having fun in our old lives; we spent all our money on feasting and frolicking. When our kids needed winter clothes, I shoplifted from stores in Rutland. Tricia spent a lot of time on the phone begging her husband and parents for money. We waitressed, cleaned hotel rooms, babysat, and tried to budget, but we were always broke.

Once, I left Joe with Tricia and her girls and drove down to Boston with a carful of other amateurs to buy a kilo of marijuana. We heard it came from Mexico by boat and was free from sticks and seeds, insuring a higher potency than what we'd been smoking. Somewhere in the supply chain the pot had been dried, pressed into bricks, and wrapped in plastic. I'd never bought pot in a brick—it was a get-rich-quick scheme dreamed up by the local ski-bum-pusher, who guaranteed we'd turn our three hundred dollar investment into a thousand dollars of profit.

In the car we had a load of fresh-rolled joints and a case of Rolling Rock to fortify us for the six-hour round trip. At our destination, I simply handed my cash to the leader of our pack, too stoned to get out of the car. We partied all the way back up Interstate 91.

I'd been smoking up since—when? Late teens? Early twenties? I have no idea. (Such is the nature of marijuana. You lose track.) I'd seen God many times, listening to Joe Cocker, the Rolling Stones, and The Doors with a mind permeated by those consciousness-raising vapors. But my foray into pot dealing withered on the vine. I smoked it all up, and shared it willy-nilly with friends and strangers alike, unable to make any kind of clear-headed money transaction.

Judy Garland had passed away that summer, felled by wine and pills; Tricia and I often laughed that we ingested more drugs and alcohol in an hour than Judy did before she ODed. The delusion of our invincibility propelled us to smoke more pot, drink more alcohol, and swallow stronger drugs.

Chapter 13

I have few memories of my sister Maere as a child. She never played with me, or even talked to me. She didn't acknowledge me on the playground, introduce me to her friends, or join in games with my friends. If I happened to pass by her in a group she would sarcastically spew "nice hair" or chant "ring around the collar" (a jingle from a TV commercial about laundry soap) for everyone's amusement. When I got my period she teased me mercilessly in front of her friends. She terrified me.

In Irish folklore there's a grey crow is called the Morrigan, a female foreteller of doom. The name Morrigan is derived from the word "maere" connoting terror or monstrousness as in nightmare. The "rigan" in mor-rigan translates as queen, as does my name, Regan. Maere-Regan equals Mor-Rigan, or the nightmarish queen. Her talons are embedded in my soul.

The Morrigan didn't invite me to her wedding.

Men and women at every age thought of my sister as having impeccable taste—at once conservative and trendy. She'd made herself known by opening a Jersey Shore clothing store for the nattily attired. All the locals shopped there, and they had high expectations for their hometown high-heeled fashion maven's wedding extravaganza.

When I heard about it in my Vermont hippie commune, I made my plans to crash the wedding.

I anointed my insulted spirit with LSD and cheap wine. In order to fund my excursion, I managed to sell some of my Boston pot, saving bits to share with friends at the Morrigan's reception. For my travels I wore a few outfits, all at the same time. (A suitcase is unwelcome when you are hitchhiking seven hours down Interstate 95.)

I'd lifted a dark, heavy wool skirt from the thrift shop in Rutland, and added green fringe on the bottom to make it ankle-length. Underneath I wore my best blue jeans, on which Tricia had embroidered red, yellow, and orange flowers with green leaves and purple vines. My tops were two long-sleeve cotton henleys, one white and one purple. Over these I wore a 1940s white silk blouse borrowed from a friend who had taken it from her grandmother's closet. It had pearl buttons, a pin-tucked collar and shoulder pads, and was darted to fit like a long toreador jacket. My overcoat was a homemade poncho, black and red wool tweed on one side, black fake fur lining on the other. I wrapped my head in a large wool flowered challis tied at the nape of my neck and draped around the front. The fringe fell freely over my chest. My feet were encased in gold-colored mountain-climbing boots with new red laces.

Small plastic bags of marijuana were tied all the way around my bra, dangling like a string of Christmas lights. I packed toiletries and extra underwear in my army surplus knapsack, along with a couple of hidden joints, a few dollar bills, and a Christmas-cookie tin of pot-laced brownies.

Two nervous guys driving directly to New Jersey's Garden State Parkway picked me up. They were delivering a stolen car to Newark, and I was afraid they might discover my dangling bags of pot and steal those too. I did what any self-respecting paranoid pot-smoker did in the sixties—I offered to share a joint. They mellowed out.

I got dropped at the Newark Airport exit on the Garden State Parkway next to a pay phone. Grateful to be alive and stoned out of my mind, I called a friend to fetch me.

St. Catherine's-by-the-Sea, a replica of St. Peter's in Rome, was the perfect backdrop for Jersey Shore's finest wedding party ensembles. I did not fit in.

At the country club reception I slipped a few of my brownies onto the dessert tray. The place turned into a free-wheeling kissing bacchanalia. I trust my gift created a most memorable wedding feast.

Maere never said a word to me. Hello. Goodbye. What are you doing here? Nothing.

As I stumbled away from the family that day, Aunt Joanne chased after me, handed over twenty dollars and begged me not to hitchhike back to Vermont.

Disconnected from my family, I fell lower and lower. My imbalanced emotional connection to the sixty percent of Americans who were against the Vietnam War drove me to protest, argue, march, drink and drug myself into oblivion. In December 1970, defeated, I collapsed, failing to escape the world of war, within and without.

Chapter 14

I couldn't see, but I heard something.

"Regan. Can you hear me? What did you take?"

"She's coming to. Be careful, she'll be agitated. She might start swinging."

I opened my eyes to an image of my mother. I wondered if time collapsed and she was in heaven with me.

The person on my right looked familiar, but she wouldn't be in heaven.

"Regan, it's Lynn. You are in the hospital." Lynn was a nurse I knew from a local watering hole where my boyfriend was a bartender. She wasn't in her uniform, and I asked what she was doing in the hospital. She was there with me.

"Me? Why?"

She raised the bed and adjusted the pillows behind my head. I looked down at myself and saw dried blood and mucous. I smelled stale booze. Someone must have had an accident. But why was it all over me?

Lynn saw the question. "They pumped your stomach," she explained quietly.

I was looking at the remains. My mother's terror-filed eyes told me she was sorry. I felt love for her, from her.

Conversations started. Lynn explained to my mother that I needed to be admitted to a psychiatric institution now that I was out of the coma. Did she have a preference? I fell asleep.

Awake again in the hospital bed, I saw my mother, some doctors, nurses, and a policeman around me. Lynn was gone. A nurse was hanging a bottle of clear liquid onto a silver hook above my head. I followed a thin plastic tube from the bottle down the side of a shiny pole over the bedrail to a bandage in the crook of my arm. Her illuminated eyes saw me cry. Don't be afraid, they said. I thought she must have been an angel helping me get on my feet to see God.

A policeman was above me. He started, stopped, and started again to tell me: the law said I attempted murder, but if I agreed to go to a mental institution, they wouldn't press charges.

To my left, my mother held a paper. I adjusted my body toward her and found a pen in my hand. I signed myself into Marlboro Psychiatric Hospital, the most disreputable public mental institution in the state of New Jersey.

As I was lifted into the ambulance I heard my mother say, "She didn't try to kill anyone but herself. This is asinine." She got in the ambulance. I fell back to sleep.

I woke shaking wet on a mattress in a small room with a window high up on a wall opposite the door. In the locked ward, I was withdrawing from my demons—booze, LSD, black beauties, hashish, mescaline, and marijuana, on top of the eighty Seconals and forty Valium I swallowed to try to kill myself. I was swaddled like a baby and couldn't move my arms. Turning my head toward the floor, I saw Mickey and Minnie Mouse, Goofy and Donald Duck dancing around the floor with musical notes and instruments. The whole gang danced up the wall and out the window. I screamed for them to come back. Someone came in, untied the straps holding me together, and gave me pills. And so at twenty-four-years old I began my recovery.

In the notorious public madhouse known as Marlboro, patients attacked one another, food-borne germs killed people, and the criminally insane were constantly plotting to escape. Alcohol and drug rehabilitation didn't exist there. My psychiatrist terrified me with photos of headless babies born to LSD-consuming mothers. Fresh out of a straitjacket, and having arrived in a hospital gown, I had no clothes or shoes of my own. I wore a short-sleeved baggy muslin dress made by the permanent residents. I shook from head to toe, broke out in hives, and vomited after every meal.

"You have a visitor," the nurse said, before escorting me from my cell-like room to the end of the hallway, and into a clean and airy space she called the Day Room. There were windows along the wall opposite the door, starting about six feet up from the floor and reaching the ceiling. For the first time, I realized my confinement was subterranean.

My father turned toward me. I hadn't seen him since the month before I entered college; he'd been wearing a dirty blue bathrobe and had been, as usual, drunk. Now he wore a brown felt fedora, soft brimmed with a hand-creased crown, and elegant duds: white open-necked shirt, tweed sports jacket, gabardine trousers, and his signature cordovan wing-tips. A miasma of feelings engulfed me. I feared him. I missed him. I loved him. I hated him.

Why didn't she say it was my father? I had no idea how to talk to him, or anyone else for that matter. I rattled into a search for some kind of appropriate words. I knew only hippie language.

"Hey, man. Far out. You're here. I'm a little strung out."

He told me his story of recovery from alcoholism.

He'd loved the effect ever since his first teenage beer. After that, once he picked up the first drink, he'd binge until he was forced to stop. He couldn't hold a job. He had been in and out of jail for getting in fights, drunken driving, and cashing bad checks.

In the end, he'd holed up in the New York apartment where I'd last seen him, drinking quarts of scotch round-the-clock until an old friend knocked on his door and said: Had enough, Burke?

After years of trying on his own, these bewitching words got him to open the door and allow a few men from Alcoholics Anonymous to enter his life. The obsession to drink lifted. "A miracle," he called it.

He told me about an AA meeting at the hospital. He didn't suggest I go, didn't offer to take me, didn't tell whoever it was that had been charged with moving me around. He just laid the words down. Then he left. He never removed his hat.

After my father's visit and the month-long stay in Marlboro, I joined Alcoholics Anonymous. When I was a few months sober I stood at the podium of a large AA meeting in Montclair, New Jersey, one of Manhattan's bedroom communities. I talked about my inability to stop drinking, stop smoking pot, stop consuming illicit drugs, until I got to AA. I was happy to be sober; I teared up with gratitude for my father who'd brought me into the Fellowship.

When I finished my talk, a line of well-wishers formed. One petite pearly lady stood back from the line before approaching me.

"I pray for you every day," she said

"What? Do I know you?"

"I go to meetings in New York with your father."

She said she and others had helped him figure out what to say before he saw me in the hospital—they'd told him to keep it simple, share his story, and suggest I go to meetings, just like they would have done with any other alcoholic.

"A lot of us," she said, "have been praying for you for a long time."

Chapter 15

Julius Roehrs Garden Center in Farmingdale hired me to make terrariums in glass bowls, a new fad. In my first job as a sober adult I spent all day planting miniature sedum and echeveria while having psychedelic flashbacks and dancing around to tunes only I could hear.

Six months out of the psych ward, I picked up the *The Exorcist* at the Main St. Drug Store after dropping my four-year-old son at his interim home with his grandparents. (We'd played at the seaside for our weekly visit, and parted cheerfully.) I drove to the Belmar Diner, ordered a grilled cheese and coke, and opened the book. An hour later I was in my Volkswagen Bus in the diner parking lot, still bewitched by the story.

The book's demon-possessed twelve-year-old protagonist? Regan.

I'd seen my name printed on report cards, paychecks, my social security card, and my driver's license; I'd seen my name in my mother's source material, Shakespeare's *King Lear*, but I'd never seen Regan in any other context. The author, William Peter Blatty, said Regan's name came from *King Lear*. Exorcist Regan's mother was an actress whose director, Burke Dennings, visited frequently and drank too many martinis. My father—whose last name was, of course, Burke—used to love martinis. Exorcist Regan lived with her mother in Georgetown. My family had lived in Georgetown.

I finished the book in the parking lot as the sun set on the Jersey Shore's Shark River Inlet, then serpentined down the road in second gear to my mother's house. An LSD flashback came upon me like the aurora borealis. The dizzying story of Regan's demon possession plundered my healing nervous system.

Agneswas, beer-soaked as usual, drifted up from oblivion as I blasted through the front door and slammed *The Exorcist* down on the coffee table.

"Who is this guy? How do you know him? Why didn't you warn me about this? How could you let me read this?"

Agnes didn't know what the hell I was talking about. An avid reader, but detached from pop culture or bestsellers, she hadn't yet read the summer blockbuster.

I told her about Regan, Burke, martinis, Shakespeare. She speculated that maybe the author was one of her younger brother's university classmates, one of the hordes of anonymous acquaintances who'd attended parties at our Georgetown home when I was a toddler.

I consulted my father in New York, who had no idea who William Peter Blatty was, although when the movie came on the scene he pretended he did.

(Years later, a friend ran into Blatty at a political event and asked him if he'd named Regan after me. My friend reported to me, word for word, Blatty's astonishing reply: "Absolutely! That name always haunted me. Who would name their little baby after one of Shakespeare's most craven females?")

In June of 1971, I turned twenty-five.

That same month, the release of the Pentagon Papers set off a firestorm of I-told-you-so outrage by Vietnam war protesters like me. All through the sixties, Washington insiders had been leaking information that the White House was lying about our involvement in the war in Southeast Asia. Anti-war organizations published newsletters and held marches screaming at the government to pull out of Vietnam; there was no good reason for us to be there. When my son was born in 1967, I started sending streams of letters and postcards to the President and Congress begging them to end the draft. I didn't want Joe growing up in a world where he might be forced to kill another mother's son.

The Pentagon Papers confirmed that Presidents Truman, Eisenhower, Kennedy and Johnson lied about why we were in Vietnam. We stayed simply to save face—refusing to admit defeat.

Troop numbers had fallen, from five hundred thousand in 1968 to one hundred and fifty-six thousand by the end of 1971, the year the Pentagon Papers were published.

And so what? The world went on. I was sober. Jim Morrison died in his bathtub in Paris. I survived *The Exorcist*, rocked out at George Harrison's Concert for Bangladesh, and rejoiced that women were allowed into the Boston Marathon.

The Pentagon Papers' exposure of the government's lying treachery slow-cooked beyond my consciousness. AA meetings seduced me with a new recipe for living, replacing the bitter brew of the wearying world. An older woman at my meetings gave me two pieces of advice:

1) Don't comment at meetings about politics, and:

2) Wear a bra.

I did both, and managed to attract a ne'er-do-well fellow AAer, ten years older.

Kurt and I found mutual interest in the fellowship of AA and a yearning for the Christian primitivism borne out of the sixties Jesus Movement. The path of my recovery incorporated counterculture social anarchism and political activism. He had no experience with the Woodstock Nation. He'd been in the military during the Korean War, and he lived off disability payments, having convinced the Veterans Administration that his alcoholism developed in the Army. Without words, we looked for ways to bridge our generational, cultural and intellectual divide with love, God and AA.

I moved in with him.

A couple of spiritual seekers invited us to a weekly fireside Bible study at a small community church. We attended Sunday services which were replete with catchy old-fashioned hymns, Bible-based sermons, the Lord's Supper, discussion groups, and Sunday school for children. I made deep friendships and found the same kind and accepting fellowship as I did in AA. But this was a whole new way of being. I'd grown up thinking sarcastic banter and raging all-night booze-fueled arguments qualified as chit chat. And now: Smart conversations about God? I was bewildered.

The Bible fellowship modeled itself on a first-century Christian church as described in *The Acts of the Apostles*; they emphasized breaking bread, teaching, gathering in a house, and raising the spiritually dead. Peopled with a mixed bag of straitlaced school teachers and business owners, students, I-saw-the-light hippies, recovering alcoholics and drug addicts, and small-time criminals, it was a perfect sanctuary for our nascent born-again Christianity. I hungered for information about God—rules and absolutes through the literal interpretation of Scripture satisfied my appetites.

We gradually replaced AA meetings with Bible fellowship.

Kurt came home from work one day, went right to the fridge, opened the door, then slammed it shut and announced, "There's no milk!"

Fighting words. Nothing grated more than to be accused of neglecting some trivial aspect of my role as a homemaker. He drank a lot of coffee with a lot of milk. Milk on display in the fridge assured him I thought of him first, had feelings for only him, loved only him.

"What have you been doing all day that you couldn't get milk?"

He really knew how to escalate things. I did too.

"I've been busy washing your clothes. Go get it yourself."

"You are a lazy selfish bitch who thinks only of yourself!"

"And you are a fucking spoiled brat! Go home to your mother if you want to be treated like a little kid!"

He grabbed my throat with his left and slugged me with his right. *Kapow!*

As he ran out the door I screamed, "Don't ever come back!" Then I realized I was bleeding.

When I got to the dentist, he asked me if I was icing my swollen lip. I grabbed the box of tissues next to the chair as I cautiously unclenched my fist to reveal my two front teeth. I didn't want to part with them. In the short bleary-eyed drive to the dentist, they'd turned into a totem, a symbol of an interrupted life, a life where men didn't punch you in the face.

I asked the dentist if he could put them back. He couldn't. He cleaned me up and told me the skin tissue was so damaged above my lip that as I got older it would collapse and wrinkle.

He wanted to file a police report. I blew my nose and said, "No. No. I don't want that."

As I was leaving, he held out my teeth and asked, "May I discard these now?"

And there went my innocence, dumped into the trash.

And yet, I didn't leave.

Joe had been living with his paternal grandparents for his kindergarten year, and in the summer he came to live with Kurt and I. Disney World had recently opened, so we read up on how to camp, then packed our newly purchased tent, camp stove, and sleeping bags into Kurt's Mustang and drove down I-95 to Orlando and the Yogi Bear Campground.

It rained. Kurt and I fought. He got drunk and disappeared.

I drove Joe the thousand miles back to New Jersey.

When Kurt showed up a few months later, we got married.

I had fond memories of going to the ocean as a child.

Once, caught by the waves, I tumbled round and round and somehow knew to go limp, relax my breath, close my eyes and not wriggle toward the sky I couldn't see. I let myself go with the flow, let the tide do what it would with my body turned-fish-turned-seashell-turned-driftwood-turned-mermaid. Sanded, winded, exhilarated and afraid, I ended up splayed out on the beach—waiting for someone to acknowledge my courage in facing the violent ocean alone and coming out alive. But they were all in their beach chairs smoking cigarettes, drinking beer, telling jokes, gossiping, hissing—the parents, the aunts, the uncles, the friends, the neighbors. And I knew I was on my own.

That was the summer my father taught me to swim on the Mantoloking beach, the summer I made friends with the ocean.

Twenty-two years later, Kurt moved me and six-year-old Joe into a flat-roofed, low-slung stucco in the tidal flatlands of Ocean Gate, where the freshwater Toms River flowed into the saltwater Barnegat Bay. The brackish brine behind our sandy backyard nourished sea life, birdlife and shore life. Kurt, raised in the working-class Ironbound neighborhood of Newark, had spent gobs of time at the Shore and had one good characteristic—he loved nature. That first summer on the Bay, he taught Joe and me to fish, crab, birdwatch, and seine.

In knee-deep water, Joe stood on one side of the seining net, his small body barely holding up a pair of swimming trunks. He gripped the net's wooden pole with both hands. Holding the other pole, I stretched the net six feet to the side of Joe. On the count of "one, two, three!" we dug our poles into the bottom and slowly pulled them through the sand, dragging the mesh to the shore and heaving it onto the beach to see what lived beneath and around our sea-shored feet. We scrambled to sort through our catch before the low-flying seabirds could snatch up any of the tasty bits, like the bottom-feeding young flounder; the bounty always also contained some variation of detritus: tangled fishing line, faded lures, pieces of Styrofoam, oyster shells, mussel shells, small rocks and pebbles. But once in a while, something special: a jellyfish, baby turtle, or blue crab.

One afternoon an osprey flew overhead, scouting. He held something flapping herky-jerky in his talons but dropped it smack on the beach in front of our seining net. Screeching like seagulls, we threw up our arms, jumped up and down, pushed and pulled each other screaming: Kurt! Kurt!

Kurt flew out of the house, grabbed a stick and an old ice chest, and lifted the six-foot rat snake into captivity. That snake lived in a glass tank in the kitchen for months before we released it back into the sawgrass.

I learned to be the mother of a boy, to face fear, and to love Mother Nature. And—whatever else was going on in my life—she loved me back.

The day of the uber fight, Joe was weekending with his grandparents.

When I realized Kurt had walked out with our joint checkbook, I raged around the house screaming obscenities.

Eventually I climbed into my VW minibus and headed to the bank to stop him from draining the account. I could only see the road ahead of me. Everything under my skin thumped uncontrollably. I found him in the parking lot slithered low in the front seat as he drove away. I floored my van and even though I slammed right into the back of his baby blue Mustang, it seemed as though I was in slow-motion. He tore out down the two-lane highway. I pursued him, crashing into him every time he slowed in the midday traffic.

Eventually the traffic cleared and I had a clear path to hang back and get up enough steam to floor it. I bulldozed him off the road, smack into a tree.

The impact forced all the doors in my VW to fly open, but otherwise there was little damage to me or my vehicle. Without looking, I turned around and drove home.

I stayed under the speed limit, parked my van with all the doors still wide open, sauntered inside, and fell into bed believing I'd killed him. I slipped into a deep sleep, relieved from all the cares of the world.

Two church elders woke me a few hours later. I was confused about what they were telling me—my memory blurred. Kurt had escaped unharmed. The elders had spoken to the police, vouched for me, and vowed to admit me to a mental institution immediately. No charges were filed. I spent three months in a Christian psychiatric residence while Joe stayed with a church family.

The marriage would last another two years.

I had no idea how to live in a clean and sober world. I craved approval of the church elders and acceptance in the church community. But the male-dominated Bible-thumping church required wives to stay with their husbands even when husbands abused and battered them.

It was based on their literal interpretation of Scripture. After all, Ephesians 5:22-24 says: "Wives, submit yourselves to your own husbands as you do to the Lord. For the husband is the head of the wife as Christ is the head of the church, his body, of which he is the Savior. Now as the church submits to Christ, so also wives should submit to their husbands in everything."

Kurt kept trying to bully me into performing like the wives he saw in his old Ironbound neighborhood. Arguments escalated into out-of-control boxing matches, then soul-crushing silence. Authoritarian church elders counseled me to return home every time I tried to escape. I was visibly bruised but submitted to the direction of the elders, believing it was God's will. Men completely controlled my life.

Rebelliousness is a stand-out characteristic of alcoholism. In the AA literature, Bill Wilson wrote: "Rebellion dogs our every step..." I had a wild, willful, criminal past that was hard to tame. I lived in constant panic, like a hooked fish gasping at the end of a pole. My only relief was to hide in the basement and binge on vodka.

Edith, a liberated survivor of multiple husbands, challenged the church elders to explain exactly what Bible passages like 1 Corinthians 11—"A woman should wear something on her head"—had to do with modern America. She steadfastly refused to abide by the male elders' requirements and wear a head covering in church. As my role model for a brief time, she taught me how to live in our extremist Christian community as a sincere provocateur who loved God.

Knowing wives were discouraged by church elders from working, Edith encouraged me to get a real estate license and work with her in a new subdivision. I trusted her counsel because she was on her third marriage; she convinced me that financial independence was the first step to freedom if I wanted to get out of mine.

I sat in the makeshift office of a planned development—half-built single family homes on acre parcels—answering phones, staffing open houses, tidying up the office, running errands. Month after month with no salary and no prospects. But I persevered, supported by Kurt's income and buoyed by Edith's words: "You only need one sale."

Then one day an inquisitive well-dressed couple drove up and parked. They happened to be black.

I ran out to greet them, showed them the model, obtained qualifying information, and walked them outside to view the plots. The couple—Princeton University professors—picked out their dream house-to-be-built, and I called the owner of the development, told him I had a buyer, and asked him to bring a contract. Not only was I going to make a few thousand dollars, but I'd be playing a bit part in integrating our all-white community.

I had been politically active since high school, and at age twenty-seven, I had no evidence to suggest that America wasn't heeding the call to social change espoused by John and Robert Kennedy and Martin Luther King, Jr. It never occurred to me that people thought any other way.

The owner arrived with a contract. But he hemmed and hawed, saying he wasn't sure he could provide the couple their tile choice, or carpet, or kitchen cabinets. Still, nothing about his interaction with this couple seemed unusually negative, at least not to me. They signed a contract contingent on later negotiations for the decor.

The whole project slowed, then halted. Edith claimed the money ran out, thanked me for my sweat equity, then found me a part-time job making stained-glass lamps.

A few months later, I stood at my mailbox reading a legal notice naming me and the owner in a civil rights lawsuit for discrimination against the black couple from Princeton. All they wanted was a house near the ocean where they could raise their boys in a good school and send them to Little League. Guilt squeezed my chest: I was complicit in killing their dream.

"This is Edith's fault," I secretly concluded.

It never went to court. One day Edith brought me a news article saying the NAACP was testing the efficacy of the Fair Housing Act of 1968 by sending couples to white neighborhoods to purchase property.

"See?" she said. "They were shills."

All I could think was: *Good for them.*

Chapter 16

Out of Grandaddy's seven children, five survived into adulthood, including my mother, Agnes, who had the misfortune to be his caretaker off and on for a few years before the end of his reign on earth. She thought having my son Joe visit for a few weeks in the summer would quell Grandaddy's attention-getting bites and barks aimed at her and her failed life.

I questioned leaving Joe alone with Granddaddy. I didn't want his tyrannical personality to rub off on my son. I chanced it because they both loved baseball.

He spent game days in his favorite chair in front of the TV with Joe at his feet. Wearing his baseball cap and casually waving a bat around, Granddaddy and Joe rooted for the venerated New York Yankees.

Every time the Yankees got a hit, Grandaddy kicked at Joe and poked him with the bat until Joe rolled around the floor in uproarious laughter igniting sparks of mutual love between them. This was a centuries old familial love untouched by the family's well-established vengeance and jealousies. When Grandaddy died, eight-year old Joe was a pall bearer and the only relative who cried. He's still a Yankees fan.

The self-actualization movement bloomed in the sixties and seventies with books such as *The Prophet*, *I'm Ok-You're Ok*, and

Be Here Now. These publications motivated me to cultivate a deeper self by rooting out my hatred for lima beans.

I tilled the soil for a backyard garden and planted the formerly detested vegetables. When they sprouted, I thought the light green shape hanging from the stem was a single bean. After a few weeks, bumps appeared under the thick skin of the seed pod. I diligently hosed away aphids, leafhoppers, and mites, but I was sure my crop was deformed. Consulting *Rodale's Basic Organic Gardening*, I learned the bumps were part of the bean apparatus— four lima beans per pod.

After a few months, I pulled the bean pods from the vines, broke them open and started eating the sun-drenched crop right there on my knees in the garden. My neighbor flew out of her back door.

"Stop! You can't eat raw lima beans! They're poison!"

Uh-oh.

Another reason to hate them. But I was determined to use lima beans to crack open the hardened interior space between "what is" and "what could be." I brought an apronful of beans inside, cooked, salted, and buttered them, and ate the day's harvest for breakfast. They were good.

I'd turned a corner. Eating the once-dreaded lima bean aerated my closed mind. It served as a gateway drug to other new experiences: breaking free from the Christian cult, my bad marriage, dead-end jobs. Throwing off this one old idea gave me courage to imagine abandoning the secluded basement with its graveyard of empty vodka bottles. Surrendering to new work as a single mother, my only job was to organize the best plan for a nine-year-old boy's future happiness by getting sober. Again.

I returned to AA unable to stop drinking, but too afraid to ask for help. I'd go to meetings, sit in the back, not talk to anyone, leave early, and go home to bed feeling victorious because I hadn't succumbed to booze. The next day, I'd be obsessed all day with drinking, and not drinking, until I ran to the liquor store. I'd feel relieved before I even opened the vodka bottle. My body, mind and soul were momentarily calmed.

It was an unbearable psychic prison. I couldn't stop drinking. During my previous downfall, I'd never even considered sobriety until I was forced into it. Now it was clear: I'd tried to control my drinking, and couldn't. There was nothing left for me but drink myself to death.

Desperation finally forced me to open up in a small AA meeting miles from home at the edge of the New Jersey Pine Barrens. I sobered up because a few people from that group sat with me every day until the obsession to drink lifted. It was February 1976.

Chapter 17

Around that time, eight-year-old Joe and I flew to Chicago for his first introduction to his grandfather in Chicago's Lake Point Tower. Joe affectionately called him Burke. My father ran his company from a sixth floor office overlooking Navy Pier, and lived on the fifty-seventh floor with a girlfriend whose name I've forgotten. Joe affixed himself to his athletic, yoga-practicing, Gucci-loafered, New-Age grandfather. I had an abysmal track record with men, so I figured my untrustworthy father would be a good role model for Joe. So it was decided: we'd move to Chicago.

Everything must go: free books! This was the ad I placed in the Toms River weekly shopper. And everything did go. We were moving from a sandy two-story cottage with a large yard to an apartment building in the middle of the nation's third largest city; I wanted nothing from the life we were leaving in the rear-view, except our scruffy dog Smoky.

But while we were packing up in New Jersey, Burke signed a lease on a North Clark Street two-bedroom for Joe and me in Carl Sandburg Village. No dogs allowed. (I've always regretted giving up Smoky; our landing would have been smoother accompanied by a dog we both loved.)

★

"We are at the point-of-no-return," Joe announced as we drove through the halfway point near the Ohio-Pennsylvania border. "We never have to see him again."

Joe became a proficient map reader on the twelve-hour journey. For him, our point-of-no-return meant salvation from Kurt and a violent alcoholic home. Right there at the halfway point I realized how damaged my little boy was, having survived the previous four years with a violent alcoholic stepfather and an untreated alcoholic mother.

It had taken 16 years, two husbands, two mental institutions, one religious cult, and two recoveries for me to get back to Chicago. Cruising onto the Dan Ryan Expressway, the Sears Tower appeared, our beacon to a better life.

"Look, Joe, we're home."

Looking up from his map, he breathed: "We're safe."

Chicago was as intoxicating at twenty-nine as the Jersey Shore was at thirteen, but for different reasons. It offered up rooms full of recovered alcoholics who showed me how to live a higher quality life. This was not a credentialed life of material possessions. It was a deep and stimulating life of intellectual and spiritual pursuits, full of hope, real friends, art, and culture.

And politics: I found in my old hometown a hotbed of activists who were out to change the world from the bottom up. Between political activity, AA meetings, the ballet, Grateful Dead concerts, and searching for a church, I was exposed to a world I had been seeking all my conscious life. Participating in city life required a sophistication that I didn't have, yet refused to admit. I made a lot of bad decisions about jobs, men, and motherhood, and learned the ways of the world.

Our car accumulated parking ticket after parking ticket in those first few weeks. After I sold it, our lives exploded in a city unexpectedly full of walkable delights: Lake Michigan, Oak Street Beach, Lincoln Park Zoo, Marshall Field's, restaurants, movie theaters, skating rinks, pinball arcades and even Ripley's Believe It Or Not. On weekends we walked to Lincoln Park Zoo, the beach, Navy Pier and the Esquire movie theater. (A couple years later, we were there when shock-jock Steve Dahl called Kentucky Fried Chicken and ordered food delivered to the American hostages in Iran. Was there a finer education for a young boy?)

About six months after we moved, Kurt called. I heard his voice and started shaking. *How did he get my number?*

He said he'd sold our house in New Jersey. "Where should I send your half of the money?"

I told him to keep it, and never call me again. Then I hung up and vomited.

Joe heard the conversation. In a fearful voice he spoke: "He can't find us, can he?"

Joe and I bought sneaker roller skates from a typical Chicago hustler at the nearby Dearborn Garden Walk street festival in early summer 1977. They were a novelty—yellow canvas shoes attached to shock-absorbent, sound-proof neoprene wheels. We skated home that day carrying our shoes.

The rest of the summer and into the fall, after school and work and on weekends, we'd skate around the Gold Coast and the Loop, charting the smoothest sidewalks, the longest ride, uphill climbs, and downhill coasts.

One October day we skated over to Navy Pier—in those days, a deserted mile-long slab of steely smelling cement shouldered by low-slung cargo sheds. There were a few joggers trotting out and back along the sun-drenched lake, a perfect two-mile run.

We chose the leeward route, the interior midway, because we noticed half-opened doors to the cargo sheds, and no workers were in sight.

"Let's go look inside," I said.

Gregarious ring-billed gulls chatted on the wing overhead. Otherwise, the place was noiseless. We skated off to a half-opened articulated overhead door, bent under, and slid through.

Our eyes adjusted to the dimly lit warehouse. Row after row of two-story high floats showcased Dumbo, clowns popping out of train cars, horses hanging over barn doors, dragons, Charlie Brown and Lucy, castles and fairies, Santa's sleigh and reindeers and Old Mother Hubbard's shoe with her big-headed children clinging to the side.

"Whoa-ho," said Joe, "this is where they store the parade floats!"

We skated under dragon's fire and around angels' wings, farther and farther into the semi-dark. It was the year of *Star Wars* and *Close Encounters of the Third Kind*, movies that put head-trip phantasms in our everyday journeys. The bang of an unseen door slamming shut brought the moribund creatures to life—or so it seemed. The two of us tacked on our skates and sailed back through the outsized flatbeds into the light to shake off the spirits of our fright.

(I later heard the old parade floats were cleared out and dumped into the defunct Riverview Amusement Park when Navy Pier was finally renovated. I hope that's true. It'd be a perfect graveyard for the ghouls on parade.)

Joe took up skateboarding the next spring and rolled around his own Chicago with friends. All of a sudden we were separate. I had no idea how to mother a boy crossing the lintel to adolescence. I dumped my skates for a bicycle and pedaled around the ever-changing Navy Pier alone. Every once in a while I'd get spooked by a mysterious *whop!*—probably the ghosts of those clowns popping out of that train car.

Chapter 18

After separating from my mother in the sixties, my father had grifted around Alcoholics Anonymous meetings in swanky neighborhoods—Manhattan, Palm Springs, Brentwood and Palm Beach—before he'd finally landed in Chicago. He dated a string of girlfriends and engaged in short contractual legal work negotiating contracts for labor unions.

He'd been sober for six or seven years when he attended Erhard Seminar Training in 1974. The movement, known as "est," was a large-group self-awareness weekend retreat founded by modern-day American guru Werner Erhard; est boosted my father's self-awareness. For a time, it satiated his spiritual unrest and ameliorated his criminal mind.

I found comfort in my father when I first moved back to Chicago. We attended AA meetings together, talked to each other every day, and shared the writings of American Buddhists Alan Watts and Ram Dass. Although "drinking the kool-aid" wasn't yet a phrase, it's the best way to describe his level of obsession with est; he attended more exclusive retreats, outdoor survival excursions, and seminars on the way to becoming an est Trainer himself. He relentlessly pursued fellow AAers, the doormen, his girlfriends, passers-by, my sisters, and me to hop on the est bandwagon.

Before long, I capitulated and trudged off to the three-day est session. The trainer coerced me into standing in the room of three hundred strangers and confronting all the bad decisions I'd made in my life, which tore my soul to shreds for years afterwards. I helplessly allowed my father to enroll Joe in est at age fourteen, and silently cheered when Joe walked out the first hour of the sixty-hour course.

With est's emphasis on the Self, my father drifted far away from his Jesuit-educated God-centered roots. His spiritual life morphed into a reliance on his interpretation of the "god within"—that we are all our own gods and are capable of directing our own lives with no outside help. This put him at odds, too, with the basic principles of twelve-step recovery, which emphasizes turning one's will and one's life over to a higher power. The Seventh Step suggests that we humbly ask God to remove our shortcomings, while the Ninth recommends making direct amends to people we've wronged, if we can do so without causing further harm. My father was unapologetic; he didn't think he had any shortcomings. He never made amends, and even preached against it.

(To this day, people in AA tell me his greatest influence on them was his constant reminder that no human power could have relieved their alcoholism, that dependence on a higher power was essential to recovery. I never knew anyone to challenge him on his illogical, contradictory philosophies.)

In October 1979, Pope John Paul II waved to my father as he flew by his fifty-seventh floor living room window in an open-door helicopter, his white robes flapping in the wind. The Pope landed in Grant Park to perform an outdoor Mass for two hundred thousand congregants. We watched the ritual on television; my father later claimed that day as his reawakening to Catholicism.

He didn't return to Sunday Mass until the est organization dissolved years later. About that time I started noticing an accelerated disintegration in his character. His live-in girlfriends changed more frequently; he concocted more and more fraudulent business deals and get-rich-quick schemes, pitted my sisters and I against each other, closed down his legitimate business, and exaggerated his wealth.

That same year, a letter slid under our door announcing Sandburg Village was converting to condominiums and I qualified for a special below-market purchase price. I attended ad hoc tenants' meetings; they led me to believe we were all getting a raw deal.

Carl Sandburg Village was an urban renewal project between Clark and LaSalle Streets from Division to North Avenue developed in the sixties by real estate mogul Arthur Rubloff. Wealthy lakefront householders were screaming for Mayor Daley to fix the rising violence spilling over from the drug-riddled, crime-infested Cabrini-Green Housing project a few blocks west. Mayor Daley's solution had been to displace hundreds of subsistence-living non-voters and build a high-rise buffer between the treasured Gold Coast neighborhood and the troubled public housing complex.

Rubloff had paid the city one dollar for the twelve city blocks of blighted property. He'd built 2,650 rental units for downtown office workers and their families. Then two Chicago financial schemers created a legal way to force renters to buy their own apartments. Rubloff seized the opportunity to convert Sandburg Village rentals to condominiums, forcing renters to purchase or leave. I joined a class action suit to fight it. We wanted to maintain our affordable rental status. Sudden media attention resulted in city-wide sympathy for us, and antagonism for Rubloff.

I testified at City Hall, supported by a new alderman, David Orr, and his friends. They were anti-machine Democrats who called themselves Progressives.

Then another letter slid under our door. Rubloff reduced the purchase price. Plaintiffs dropped from the lawsuit. I held out. It was the right thing to do, but not alone. All my neighbors wanted to buy, and my suit held them up. Rubloff threatened to raise the price. People phoned and threatened to drum me out of town if I didn't drop the suit. Perfectly nice people yelled at me in the supermarket. Nasty letters appeared under my door. I held out.

Rubloff filed a million-dollar lawsuit against me for obstructing sales. He found a way around my lawsuit, and eighty percent of the apartments sold within ninety days. Eventually my father bought my unit—it was, after all, a good deal.

Rubloff dropped the lawsuit against me. But for years afterwards whenever I met a new Sandburg owner, they'd recognize my name, "Oh you. Your lawsuit is a cloud on my title."

From Lake Point Tower's third floor three-acre resident-only garden, I peered through my binoculars out over Navy Pier to the Harbor Lighthouse by the lock at the mouth of the Chicago River. My father, clad in Gucci swimming trunks, was striking a favorite yoga pose—standing on his head within sight of all the bathers and sun worshipers around the nearby pool. His latest girlfriend sauntered up behind me in her high-heeled sandals and gossamer brown bikini, followed my gaze and said, "I fucked someone out there once." I instantly sensed that this, my favorite spot in all Chicago, would be tainted for the rest of my life.

The woman, a reformed prostitute matriculating at the University of Chicago, had just moved in with my father, who seemed quite proud of his latest catch. She and I were about the same age, thirty-three. I'd go to AA meetings and celebrate the yearly anniversary of my last drink; meanwhile she'd celebrate her own reformation by announcing her milestones to us, such as: "It's been 90 days since my last trick." They had a few things in common, including their food intake, which they discussed constantly. Avid devotees of the Dr. Atkins' low-carbohydrate diet, they packed their fifty-seventh-floor fridge with a lot of white protein—cottage cheese, plain yogurt, eggs, chicken, tuna salad— plus sugar-free Vernor's ginger ale. They disdained calorie counting (though she secretly kept a chart) and instead tracked protein grams and carbohydrates.

The Atkins diet was all the rage in Alcoholics Anonymous. My father cornered newcomers and hammered a Dr. Atkins wedge into their soggy brains before jotting down his phone number and saying, "Call me anytime." Whenever he saw someone at an AA meeting holding a donut, he'd explain that a no-sugar low-carb diet keeps the blood sugar regulated and, in turn, reduces the craving for alcohol. Beginners were known to eat all-protein tuna fish right out of the can, in accordance with his dictates.

The grocery store on the second floor of his building had a deli counter with a superior version of my favorite food, cole slaw. Not too long after the day on the terrace, I purchased a pint each of cole slaw and tuna fish salad and rode up to their apartment.

The kitchen counter was strewn with the maniacal makings of another high protein drink. Next to the bartender-grade electric mixer stood pricey containers from Sherwyn's Health Foods: powdered desiccated liver, brewer's yeast, magnesium, Vitamin C, flax seed, liquid amino acids, sunflower oil, and liquid lecithin. (A brown substance that could lubricate a car.) The former prostitute was there, too. "Don't let your father see you eating that cole slaw," she said. "It's loaded with carbs."

I knew this no-sugar, no-mayo cole slaw was not, in fact full of carbs, but she generally scared the hell out of me, so I hid the offensive food in the closet until I left for home.

She, like those before and after her, looted the towels when she split, but left the expensive stuff on the kitchen counter. He binged on coffee Häagen-Dazs for a few days before resuming his anti-social eating habits. I brought him new white towels from Crate and Barrel.

A few months later, my father called. A woman he'd met in AA was homebound after surgery.

"Can you go over and see if you can help out?" he said.

The woman opened the door to her lakefront apartment looking like someone had bashed her face in.

"On my God, what happened to you? Did you get mugged?"

"Oh no, I had my nose fixed. I guess I look pretty bad."

A nose job? He had me visit her because she had *a nose job*?

She proceeded to direct me to the bathroom as if I had been hired as a visiting hairdresser; I proceeded to wash her mane, which was about twenty years younger than mine. The long thick ash blonde curls took forever to rinse in the bathroom sink. The whole time I wondered if she'd had her arms fixed too, and that's why she couldn't wash her own hair. When she asked if I'd help with the dishes, I said I had to go.

Her move-in, move-out with my father lasted a few months. She took the towels when she left. A few years later she married an age-appropriate man. My father had my son deliver two dozen long-stem yellow roses to her.

In the late 1970s a group of small investors formed a joint venture to buy an old residential hotel at the corner of St. Clair and Ontario. They hired me to help them relocate the residents and keep the operation rolling until they sold it.

Most residents had the kind of money to allow them to live elsewhere, but the rundown month-to-month existence at the Eastgate suited them just fine. A few had checked into the hotel in the 1940s and just stayed on. After one mink-clad, cigarette-smoking woman moved to a nursing home, the housekeeper appeared in front of me doubled over in laughter. When she cleaned the octogenarian's room, she found a dresser drawer full of dildoes. Another man left behind a trunkful of old drug paraphernalia, including glass syringes.

I learned quite a bit about the hotel business, especially it came time to sell. One of the owners, a contractor with a lien on the property, had an office on the second floor. He was supposed to accumulate all the documents necessary for the sale, but he was short on business acumen, and most of the work fell on me. The day of the closing, he and I were to meet at the hotel and haul all the papers to a LaSalle Street law office. There was a blizzard. He lived in the far suburbs and couldn't dig out of his driveway. In the conference room full of lawyers, accountants, real estate consultants, clerks, and the new owners, I showed up with the documents and had all the answers about the property. The new owners hired me on the spot.

A lawyer (or was he an accountant?) called a few days later asking me to lunch to celebrate. I showed up at a fancy hotel restaurant expecting the crowd from the day of the closing. But it was just the two of us. And he was married.

At the end of lunch, he reached across the table, touched my hand and said he had a room upstairs.

"I don't believe in adultery," I said.

"Well," he said, "let's call it something else."

For some reason I thought that was one of the funniest things I'd ever heard. Before long we were eating lunch regularly in hotel restaurants and spending time upstairs. I craved the attention, the caring, the comfort. And every Sunday morning at church I'd sit in my pew pleading with God to give me the courage to call it quits. I thought I had to tread lightly. He never indicated he'd do anything to harm me, but he had a lot of influence, and I was afraid he'd jeopardize my job.

In AA I was slowly learning sobriety is more than physical abstinence. Emotional sobriety is as important, and as hard to achieve. It requires a moral reckoning. At the end of every day, I'd be resolute in quitting this man, this torment, this threat to my sobriety. In the morning I couldn't wait to hear his voice.

Chapter 19

A journalist friend, Paul Galloway, made arrangements for me to volunteer on Adlai Stevenson III's 1982 gubernatorial campaign against Jim Thompson. Paul wrote political features for the *Chicago Sun-Times* and knew the campaign press secretary. It's best to have a reference when volunteering on a campaign or you'll get stuck answering phones, or standing on a street corner passing out pamphlets. No one trusts someone no one sent.

Senator Gary Hart gave a dazzling keynote speech at a fundraising dinner for Adlai. They were the generation of new ideas, new leadership. But I was distracted looking around the ballroom for various women I'd heard had slept with Hart. In the days leading up to the gala, I'd helped organize seating charts as a volunteer in the Stevenson campaign office. Savvy organizers more than once blurted out, "Oh you can't seat her there—they had an affair!"

I was entrusted with driving Adlai's wife Nancy around to her scheduled events. I've never known any two people as funny as Paul Galloway and Nancy Stevenson. At the end of every day, I'd have hilarious conversations with Paul recapping the day's events. He'd brief me on the day's news stories I'd missed while I was out on the campaign trail. Once in a while he'd relay bits of salacious gossip, things he'd overheard in the news room about the sex life of Adlai's opponent, Jim Thompson; I always immediately relayed these tidbits to Nancy.

Paul was writing an article on the candidates' wives, and we scheduled a day with him on the trail with Nancy. One of our stops was a Meals-on-Wheels site in Chicago's Hegewisch neighborhood. Nancy walked around the lunch room, said hello to each person individually, then started her stump speech.

"You know, my husband, Ad, voted for this Meals-on-Wheels program when he was a senator."

Before she could get out another word, a large woman in the corner yelled out: "Yeah? Well, he oughta be here now for the corned beef! 'Cause it stinks!"

By the time we dropped Nancy off at the end of the day, we were doubled over with laughter, barely able to recover from the previous sidesplitting eight hours.

When the article appeared a few days later, a campaign staffer asked if we had given Paul an aphrodisiac; the story, he said, was less of an objective feature, and more of a love letter to Nancy Stevenson.

Alas, Thompson eked out a narrow victory in November. But the margin— five thousand votes, or less than one per cent—was small enough that Adlai decided to mount a recount. In order to present his case to the Illinois Supreme Court for a statewide recount, he needed a discovery recount which required volunteers from both sides to examine a portion of ballots cast in a small number of towns throughout the state.

All my Stevenson campaign friends went immediately to work on Rich Daley's mayoral campaign against Jane Byrne and Harold Washington. Since I was unemployed and diverting my attention away from the crushing emotional bottom of another failed relationship, I accepted the job coordinating Adlai Recount volunteers for Chicago. Soon I was also responsible for Cook County suburbs, and then DuPage County as well. Volunteers from opposing camps sat side-by-side looking for voter intent on punchcard ballots. "Hanging chads" were constantly in question.

The recount came to a screeching halt in mid-December. We had arrived at the DuPage County Courthouse with our volunteers and lawyers, only to be told by the election chief that they had thrown away the all the election day computer tabulations. So we had no way of comparing ballots to election day precinct totals.

Jim Thompson went to the governor's office.

One of the Stevenson friends hired me in the marketing department of his company, Pullman Construction. It was on the far south side, at 95th & Stony Island, at a high salary; corporate benefits included a new Buick. My job consisted of scouring trade publications to procure government contracts, generating responses to Requests For Proposal, and helping to organize bid packages. I was the only female in the sales department, and although everyone was exceptionally kind to me, I sat alone in my cubicle all day. At lunch I would drive over to Calumet Park on the lake, read a book, and watch the birds from a park bench. We won a bid from the Navy to build a facility on a barely-there atoll in the Indian Ocean, Diego Garcia.

Every few nights after work, I'd drive to Daley's Bridgeport neighborhood to join friends at a one-hundred-person phone bank for Rich Daley. We changed the callers' script every day either to ask voters to support Daley, or attend a Daley event, or sign up to volunteer. Some scripts asked specific confidential polling questions.

One night a friend called from campaign headquarters.

"Jane Byrne is having an event tomorrow night at senior building on the north side. Get out the sheets from that building and call all the residents to say she cancelled. Use callers you trust."

"Ok," is all I said.

The next day's news reported the disorganized Byrne campaign forgot to tell residents she was coming, and her event was empty. None of us ever questioned the morality of such dirty tricks, especially after Byrne finished ahead of us in the primaries. Such is the nature of competitive campaigns.

You lose your virtue.

I was in good company, at least.

My father's moral drift had accelerated after those early years of sobriety and growth. He was indeed his own god, unencumbered by moral obligations or the consequences of his actions.

By the eighties he'd established a semi-legitimate business, Great Lakes Coal Company, headquartered in Chicago. As a coal broker he organized small Indiana coal operators to deliver coal to midwestern Budweiser plants. Little by little, independent coal companies were bought up by conglomerates like Peabody Coal. Eventually the conglomerates undercut the price offered by the remaining companies. Budweiser grabbed a better deal and reneged on their contract. Great Lakes Coal Company faced certain ruin.

What did he do next? He bought a coal field on a railroad spur south of Terre Haute. Loan guarantees from the State of Indiana paid for equipment to strip and haul the coal from the land. Once he had the equipment financed, he had leverage to obtain bank loans for mining operations. He negotiated a contract with an Indiana power plant and was back in business, delivering his own coal.

The price of coal dropped in the eighties, and when he could no longer make a profit, he shut down the company, deeded the coal field to an employee, and walked away from his financial responsibility to the State of Indiana. With the help of a high-powered Chicago attorney, he concocted a scheme to defraud the banks holding his loans, starting by hiding his assets in a trust.

I was named one of the beneficiaries, as well as the trustee.

My father directed me, as the trustee, to stash five hundred thousand in a Canadian bank he'd found for this purpose, and to invest two hundred and fifty thousand with his broker. I signed a lot of legal documents, having no clue what the consequences of my own actions might be. He bragged to me and his closest friends how he was getting away with cheating his creditors, the State of Indiana, and the IRS. Breaking laws came easy with the aid of a LaSalle Street attorney. I trusted that he'd keep me from legal harm. I secretly feared he'd harm me in other ways, however, if I didn't go along with his scheme—by cutting me off, not from his money, but from his approval.

The next year I saw Gary Hart deliver a speech at the University of Chicago about reforming the military. Unlike most Democrats at the time, he was not simply interested in cutting its budget; his idea was to have an educated military, trained in military tactics and history. This appealed to my anti-militarism leftover from the sixties.

When he announced his candidacy for president in late 1983, Gary Hart supporters in Chicago were hard to find. Then he came in second in Iowa.

Hearing the news on that raw midwestern evening at the end of January 1984, I hurried to the makeshift campaign headquarters from my job on the south side to help answer the phone calls bombarding the office. I met Barb Guttman, a long-time political operative; we volunteered every night working the phones to build support for Hart in Illinois. He smashed conventional wisdom by winning in New Hampshire at the end of

February, beating former Vice-President Walter Mondale. I left my corporate job and turned in my Buick to work in the three-week Illinois campaign.

Overrun with media, volunteers, and supporters looking for signs and buttons, the campaign moved from a second floor graphic arts office on artsy Wells Street to an elegant empty space in the classy downtown Monadnock Building. The campaign headquarters in Washington dispatched organizers to Chicago for get-out-the-vote and election day activities leading to the mid-March primary. Surrogate speakers arrived from all over the country before we could even schedule them into events.

One of Hart's Chicago friends, a wealthy socialite, insisted we organize a rally at a downtown hotel with her special guest: Robert Redford. With only four days to build a crowd, I called every woman in my address book.

"Hi, Marcie? Robert Redford will be here for Gary Hart on Friday."

"No, I'm not kidding. Come early and stand up front. You'll get to meet him, shake his hand. Bring friends. And a camera."

"Really. I am not kidding. Will you be there?"

The socialite secreted Redford into the holding room in a hallway closed off from the main event. He would not shake hands or sign autographs, she said. *Gulp*. He'd simply deliver his speech, introduce Hart and leave.

The hotel manager came to me with an emergency phone call. Gary Hart had just delivered a speech at Notre Dame. The South Bend airport was snowed in. He'd be driving to Chicago. His Washington-based traveling staff said it would take about three hours. I knew better. The lake-effect snow on Lake Michigan's eastern side would grind them to a halt. We'd be lucky if he got there at all. And they'd never stop at a pay phone to call the hotel with updates.

Catastrophe.

I banged on the door and yelled through the sliver of an opening the socialite allowed me. Robert Redford pushed her aside and ushered me into the holding room. I gasped for air. My legs wobbled and my already shaky voice rattled out the bad news. Redford invited me to sit down, gave me a glass of water, and asked for the lowdown on the event. I couldn't look at him.

"You'll walk into the room at stage right, three hundred supporters behind a rope line, a stage with two steps up and microphone, three TV stations with cameras, and four print reporters. No one expects interviews."

I didn't mention most of the attendees were women.

And Robert Redford said, "How 'bout I go out and kill time signing autographs?"

Barb Guttman had gathered other volunteers and friends at the perfect spot to get a handshake. When I walked in with Robert Redford, they screamed. I almost screamed with them. He walked right up to our group, shook hands, and posed for photos. After he finished signing autographs, he hopped on the stage and said how great Gary Hart was, particularly in his work for clean air and water. He worked the room again, went out the door and said to let him know when I heard from Hart.

There was no way to know where the Hart group was as they rounded the bottom of the Lake through northern Indiana into Chicago. I could only tell people he was on his way. By the time he arrived the curious political operatives, and all the press who'd gathered to hear him, had left. They were disappointed. Not me though.

Nor my friends.

We had Robert Redford.

★

Gary Hart lost the Illinois primary, and I joined the Hart for President "road warriors," an idealistic band of unpaid and broke true believers. We traveled together to Missouri, then Indiana for the final Midwestern primary. I went on to the Washington headquarters to work as a scheduler for the few months before the Democratic Convention in San Francisco.

Hart and the entire staff flew to California on the last charter plane the campaign could afford. I sat next to the campaign's issues director, who was reading *Notes From The Underground*. When Hart passed by us, he pointed to Phil's book.

"Great book. I've read all of Dostoevsky," Hart said.

Phil whispered to me, "No wonder we're losing, Americans hate intellectuals."

Hart had won enough delegates overall to qualify for seats at the convention. The other Hart delegates and organizers and I hustled around the convention floor trying to persuade Mondale delegates to switch their votes to Hart.

"All the polls show Hart has a better chance to beat Reagan," I insisted. "You'd better vote for him if you want a Democrat in the White House."

They didn't budge.

Walter Mondale won the Democratic nomination and went on to win the District of Columbia and his home state of Minnesota. Ronald Reagan took every other state.

"I'm done with Chicago," my father told me sometime that fall. "I can't stand living in a town where a queer black man is the mayor." He'd repeat that sentiment, adding crude modifiers with increasing force to admiring friends over the phone. "There's nothing here for me anymore."

I knew this open disdain for Chicago was all part of his con, but that last proclamation stung. I wondered if any of his friends confronted him with, "What about Regan and Joe?"

I'd never heard my father speak unkindly toward any black or gay man. He'd always charmed them with his well-dressed, well-mannered air of significance, in much the same way he presented himself to both bank presidents and bikini-clad sunbathers. When Harold Washington had been running for mayor, my father had never expressed prejudice or bigotry of any kind about him. But my father was obsessed with saving face, not from family and friends, but from future marks. So now that Washington was in charge, my father concocted this sudden hatred for him, and used it as his excuse to get out of town before the creditors closed in and exposed him. He seemed to embrace his manufactured prejudice. He knew his wealthy friends would nod in solidarity. And they did.

Perhaps that is the genesis of all bigotry—the need to hide from a completely unrelated truth.

Like cheating your creditors.

After a month of dodging creditors and process-servers in Chicago, he called me from Caesar's Palace in Las Vegas, excited to lay out his newest plan. He'd pretended to gamble away his money; this would provide an alibi to bank investigators as to why he was broke.

Since Florida homestead laws protected homeowners from creditors, he flew there next and bought a condominium in the Palm Beach Biltmore overlooking the Inland Waterway. As for packing up and moving his Chicago possessions? That was left to his new wife and her son.

Chapter 20

I was working on Adlai Stevenson III's second gubernatorial campaign when a fellow staffer and I met him at Berghoff's Restaurant to brief him on his speech at the 1986 Illinois AFL-CIO convention. He was already seated with a martini.

The AFL-CIO had endorsed Adlai four years earlier during his losing campaign against Jim Thompson. As governor, Thompson had agreed to legalize collective bargaining for the state employee union, a major victory for the union and state workers. By the time Thompson's reelection rolled around, unions had broken their traditional bond with Democrats and endorsed the Republican governor.

We needed labor unions' support. Adlai was running on the Solidarity Party ticket; he needed the forces of friendly union members to fan out around the state and educate confused Democratic voters. (Adlai had formed the Solidarity Party because right-wing followers of Lyndon LaRouche had won two spots on the Democratic ballot in the primary. Adlai, repulsed by the LaRouchies' conspiracy-ridden statements, refused to be on the Democratic ticket with them.)

On this September evening Adlai would present his labor union bona fides and make the unusual plea to the rank-and-file to vote for him even though their leaders had endorsed his opponent.

Adlai kept up his busy daily law practice while campaigning for governor, so we were accustomed to briefing him either in his office at lunchtime, at the end of the workday, or in the car on the way to his evening campaign events. Or (as was the case today) at Berghoff's, his favorite Loop restaurant.

When the waiter took our dinner orders, Adlai ordered another martini, a steak, baked potato and a salad. We ordered nothing. We had a lot of ground to cover, and food and drink would be in the way. When the second martini arrived, Adlai asked for beer with dinner.

The campaign's fast-talking issues director, David Oskandy, laid out the parts of the speech. He emphasized important transitions, including the obligatory laugh lines—which didn't seem that funny to me. Our press secretary presented the anticipated media questions Adlai might have to answer after the speech—especially those having to do with Adlai's recent off-the-cuff remarks where he'd mused about replacing unionized highway workers with prison inmates. My part as the campaign scheduler was to familiarize Adlai with last minute changes to the schedule, review the personalities and politicians who'd be at the event, and give him an estimate of how many rank-and-file Stevenson supporters with "Labor for Adlai" signs would be in the audience.

Adlai listened as he ate his dinner. He ordered another beer. The three of us interrupted and contradicted each other, talked frantically fast, repeated ourselves, and got louder and louder—feeling like we had to race against the clock, although there was plenty of time before the evening's event.

After dinner Adlai ordered a brandy, sat back in his seat, and asked questions of each of us. And as informed as we all were, we had no answers to his questions. He proved to us, as he always did, that he had an unmatched intelligence, with a mind that absorbed information, clicked through and organized it, then rolled it out with high-caliber vocabulary, and ideas that few understood.

He savored his Irish coffee as he held forth on the history of labor unions, and the Stevenson family's complicated legacy with them.

The press secretary gave the signal that it was time to hit the road. Adlai stumbled to his feet and muddled through thank-yous and goodbyes. David and I locked eyes in terror.

We slumped on the table. Finally, David ordered his own martini and said, "Oh well. No one ever understands what he's saying anyway."

The Stevenson campaign treasurer was Herb Sirott, an absolute gem of a man.

Herb often strolled lithely to work in Italian tweed and leather, crisp-not-starched shirt and continental-not-old-school tie, walking from his Lake Shore Drive condo to his law office in the Loop. Sometimes he wore an overcoat, never buttoned, flapping like cherub wings at his side. He was the stranger everyone acknowledged and smiled back at as he stooped to buy a newspaper, waved to doormen, or handed a few bucks to his street buddies like the outsider artist who lived on the steps of the Water Tower.

Herb solved multiple legal problems for every unashamed credit risk in his path. They found him in the coffee line, in the seat next to him at the movies, at the barber shop, riding an elevator. He was incapable of turning anyone away. Herb's atheist higher power infused him with unshakable compassion.

Chicago had started opening its sidewalks to cafes, and Herb had taken to living outdoors. Every Sunday I found him draped over cappuccino and *The New York Times* in heavy discussion with his wife, Vivienne. He'd read every word in William Safire's "On

Language" column out loud to us. Consuming neither alcohol nor meat, Herb never judged those who did; he welcomed all characters, oddballs, famous and infamous, educated or not into his cafe society on Chicago sidewalks.

Herb often came to the headquarters after hours to deliver paychecks and soak in the hum and buzz of mobilized politics. Despite being a vegetarian, he frequently bought everything-on-it pizza for us staffers who had forgotten to eat all day. He quietly slipped cab fare into the hands of poorly paid women whose late-night campaign work spilled over into the danger zone for public transportation.

After the derailment by the LaRouchies, the campaign was in a twilight zone. There was no way Adlai's Solidarity Party would win in Illinois, but in order to do our jobs we all had to pretend we were winning. Delirium seemed to rule each day. Everything was either exaggeratingly funny or weepingly sad. We were at our best and our worst.

Adlai lost by four hundred thousand votes. Given the circumstances, it felt like a victory.

Chapter 21

Thank God for rock-and-roll. I would have hated trucking through life with the likes of Frank Sinatra or Ella Fitzgerald. I need backbeat. My baby-boom generation was defined by its music; we had the purchasing power to buy our own, in the form of ten-cent 45 rpm records. As a pre-teen I'd cobble together loose change and ride my bike to the comic-book store in Wilmette's No-Man's-Land for the latest 45s of Elvis, Bill Haley, Buddy Holly and Martha and the Vandellas.

Portable transistor radios had been on the scene in 1954, and two years later when Elvis Presley gave us "Hound Dog," my ten-year-old ears heard simple fun lyrics. The looks adults exchanged whenever Elvis came on the radio ignited my curiosity, however. These people knew something I didn't. I was determined to figure out what it was. The more I bopped around singing "Hound Dog," the more I understood. They thought they were high-class, but that was just a lie. Yeah, I was on to them.

Armed with the revelation that I was smarter than my elders, I'd started running my own life. I did what I wanted, went where I wanted, and wore what I wanted. I danced into middle age still listening to this anthem of self-will—in the relationships I pursued, and the politicians I supported. And I suffered an onslaught of syncopated consequences.

The Talking Heads movie and album *Stop Making Sense* had come out in 1984, when my son Joe was seventeen. Joe and I had been movie companions our whole lives, but he'd had to talk me into this one, which debuted in Chicago at the Fine Arts theater on Michigan Avenue. "I'm not into punk rock," I told him.

Fortunately he assured me it was anything but. We'd sat in the darkened theater as lead singer David Byrne appeared on screen, jerking across the stage in an oversize white boxy suit, a confusing mix of hip, new age, and classic.

When Byrne white-sneakered up to the mic to sing "Psycho Killer," Joe leaned over to me and said, "That takes a lot of guts." I knew what he meant. Joe, living on his own, had formed a band, Lost Cause. They were about to appear on stage for the first time at the Metro, Chicago's iconic showcase for young bands. Life for him was all about guts.

And now, a few years later, Gary Hart had set up his campaign headquarters for a second run at the presidency. I quit another secure job, packed all my belongings in a new car, slipped *Talking Heads* into the cassette player, and drove to Denver to work as the Hart campaign's political director for the Midwest.

Granted, I had another reason to leave town: my on-again, off-again romance with the married man, the one I'd met after the hotel sale. I couldn't stay away from him and couldn't stay with him. I'd break it off, for months at a time. He'd eventually be parked outside my building as I headed out to work. I'd accept a ride, giggle at his jokes, make plans for lunch, and it would start all over again. He was as hard to stay away from as alcohol and drugs ever were. I was accumulating more secrets and lies than I could bear. Pleading with God to lift me from the powerless obsession, I sang "Take Me To The River" nonstop for fifteen hours west on Interstate 70. When I arrived in Denver for the cause, I felt cleansed.

New York Governor Mario Cuomo was the biggest threat to Hart winning the primary. When Cuomo withdrew from the race in February 1987, Hart was the clear frontrunner. All the polls showed him beating Republican Vice President George Bush.

In May, fifty-one-year old Gary Hart took a trip to Bimini. Within a week the *Miami Herald* had a photo of a twenty-nine-year old beauty draped on his lap onboard the yacht, *Monkey Business*. Though gossip about women followed Hart everywhere, the Denver campaign office tried to believe he would never have so carelessly jeopardized the presidency—or the lives and careers of all of us who'd moved there from all around the U.S. to work for him.

Hart tried to conduct a normal campaign, but after a week of hounding from the media for answers to questions about his extramarital affairs, he dropped out of the race. The campaign manager hastily delivered paychecks to the staff with instructions to leave the office and cash them immediately. He feared vendors would seize the campaign's assets.

I left the office, went to the bank, then headed to a standing-room-only downtown AA meeting. The chairperson asked if anyone was from out of town.

"My name is Regan. I'm an alcoholic from Chicago," I said. "Came to work for Gary Hart."

The room erupted in laughter. Good old AA, reminding me to wear life like a loose garment. After the meeting someone offered me a job. I laughed, but my innards were fluttering like hummingbird wings. Nothing around me seemed close enough to touch. Everything in front of me and everything far away seemed blurred.

Barb Guttman flew from Chicago for a few days to escort me through deteriorating mental functions. I sat on the couch staring at dust particles floating in sunshine streams. Every few hours I'd walk around weeping and kicking stuff. She interrupted my cognitive disturbance by asking if I'd like to eat, and suggesting it might be time to call the movers.

Eventually I packed up my car, slammed *Talking Heads* in the cassette player, cranked up the volume and wailed to the music all the way back home.

I headed off to Indianapolis to manage an unpromising U.S. Senate campaign. I should have gone home to Chicago to look for a job there instead.

Six months later, Gary Hart changed his mind and started working his way back into the race. The day before Thanksgiving I was contacted by a reporter from the *Gary Post-Tribune* for a comment about the rumor that Hart was getting back in.

My friend Roger Ebert, a newspaperman for the *Chicago Sun-Times*, had always cautioned me in my political work to never talk to the press. "You'll just screw yourself," he said. "They're out to trip you up. Just say 'No comment.'"

I had heeded his advice religiously up until that point. But I was on my way out the door—headed, coincidentally enough, to Roger's vacation house in Michigan. I'd been invited to his legendary Thanksgiving party, and all I was thinking about were the days ahead, which promised great food, real characters and loads of laughs. In other words, this particular reporter had caught me off guard. I told him my honest thoughts and headed out, without giving the phone call a second thought.

Roger Ebert loved people. He'd purchased successively bigger houses in Michigan to accommodate weekend guests. During those weekends we'd take caravan excursions to the used book store in Niles, and to art and antique stores in Lakeside. At home we'd play poker and watch movies. In his well-stocked kitchen everyone chipped in to make big family-style meals. Roger told the same funny stories over and over. I was his biggest audience and his biggest target. He teased me relentlessly about all my losing campaigns.

"If you want to place winning bets on who's going to lose, find out who Regan's working for," he'd say.

On that Saturday, Roger returned from the store in New Buffalo with newspapers, bagels and cream cheese. Someone brewed up a pot of coffee, and the weekenders gathered at the big old dining room table. All of a sudden Roger screamed that I was on the front page of the *Gary Post-Tribune*. When he read the quote aloud, he laughed so hard he could hardly spit it out.

My quote about Gary Hart: "It's his swan song. This is like a lover who woos you, then dumps you, then comes back, asks forgiveness, woos you again and dumps you again. I'm not falling for it."

I never lived it down. The more embarrassed I got, the more Roger loved telling it. For the rest of the day, all the next day, and nearly every time I saw Roger for years afterwards he recited my quote.

Gary Hart did get back in the race. And I did help him get on the ballot in Illinois. He got four percent of the vote in New Hampshire, then dropped out again.

My candidate in Indiana lost, too.

But I had given Roger one big priceless punch line.

R.I.P. Roger. We miss you.

Chapter 22

Having failed to keep the Indiana campaign afloat—we'd had no money, and only one other staffer—I walked out. Depressed, anemic and ashamed, I beat a hasty retreat to a cousin's vacation house in the Bahamas, where she would join me in time with her husband and two small children.

My plane landed at the North Eleuthera International Airport and slid right off the short runway. Looking down from my window seat I was horrified to see the tropical brush getting churned up and blown outward by the small prop plane. The passengers exploded into hoots and hollers after we'd lurched to a full stop. *Were we safe?*

"Don't worry!" yelled the pilot. "This happens all the time. The sand blows onto the runway and makes it slippery."

He backed up onto the tarmac, and the door of the plane opened to a rush of fragrance. *Roses? Coconut? Ginger?*

"That's frangipani," said the flight attendant. "You'll smell it everywhere."

Station wagon taxis drove us fifty-miles-an-hour on the sandy one lane road to the water-taxi dock. The lush wide-leaf vegetation shouldering the road slapped so hard against the car it sounded like we were bulldozing through mile-high cornfields. At the dock the stink of wet gaseous pulp arising from the surrounding mangrove trees made me gag. Gasoline and oil from the idling water taxis stirred up into the tropical air. Fellow passengers and I boarded the small canopied motorboat with our suitcases full of clothes we'd never wear.

We sped off toward tiny seventeenth century Dunmore Town, a garden hamlet of pink, yellow and blue colonial houses weighed down by old-vine bougainvillea and hurricane-battered palm trees. Saltwater sprayed our welcoming faces and dried out our pollution-soaked nostrils. The sun heated, then soothed the top of my head, melting my icy restlessness.

Happy-faced Bahamians in faded flowery shirts greeted us on the crowded town pier, full of cars and trucks awaiting passengers and goods from the mainland. I shouted to the gathering on the pier, "Sunsets? Anyone going to Sunsets?" The islanders pointed toward Otis, the driver. On the two-mile drive from the town pier, speeding in Otis's Volkswagen Van on another low sandy road through more high vegetation and palm trees, I realized I'd never before been in a tropical country. Otis talked non-stop in rhythmic Bahamian, as soothing as a Bob Marley tune.

Sunsets, a three-bedroom lime green cottage, fronted the bay between Harbour Island and Eleuthera. From the water's edge, I could barely make out the boats crossing from the town pier to the airport water-taxi landing. No other boats were visible on the late afternoon bay, famous for shallow-water bonefishing.

I claimed my room, unpacked, and sat outside listening to the sound of nothing. No news. No poll numbers. No bad press. No men behaving badly.

In the following days, I lounged in a hammock between two rubber trees reading James Michener's *Caribbean*. While snorkeling in undulating salty turquoise under cloudless skies, I kept a slow pace with the barracuda, sea turtles, starfish, octopus and shoaling bonefish—hyper-aware of every movement, every flutter, every splash.

The day Therese and her family were to arrive, I took an early walk in the pink sand, harvested sand dollars, picked avocados, papayas and mangoes for lunch, and fell asleep on the terrace overlooking the stilled Eleuthera Bay.

An unearthly, ominous pounding reverberating from the driveway woke me. I rushed around back and found Therese's three-year-old daughter Melissa jumping up and down on the roof of their car. When the jumping jack saw me she screamed, "There's my cousin Regan!"

Sweet paradise, I was a happy camper.

After a supper of grouper and coconut bread, we stretched out face-up on Sunsets' dock, feeling the earth turn away from the sun and listening to the soft ripple of the sea creatures settling in for the night. An unfamiliar billion-star sky was our evening entertainment.

The frangipani and bay breezes lulled me into a rare undisturbed sleep. In the morning I heard Therese in the kitchen packing food and drinks for a day at the beach. Everyone grabbed a towel. I took five-year old Peter's hand and we all walked to the top of the sandy road, hiked through a small pine grove and down to the pink sands of the Atlantic Ocean. Wading in baby blue water as tropical fish swam around our legs, we collected coral, sea shells and sand dollars. We picnicked on the beach and half slept in the warm sand.

When Therese and her family ended their vacation, I remained in the cottage for another five months. AA meetings in the old wooden school were attended by Bahamians, tourists and sailors who lived on their boats and came in from the sea each week. The local regulars were my companions. I had a torrid affair with an islander, scuba dived with an oceanographer, and practiced yoga with international expats. At the end of August, I ran out of money and returned to Chicago, flushed with island fever.

I'd gotten a call in the Bahamas from Illinois Speaker Michael Madigan's chief of staff, a call that landed me on a campaign for a state representative. Democrat Clem Balanoff was challenging incumbent Sam Panayotovich, who had defected to the Republican Party along with his pal Fast Eddie Vrdolyak. The legislative district included the shuttered steel mills and leaking landfills of Chicago's industrial southeast side.

The Balanoff family were union-organizing, buck-the-machine Progressives who lived along the Illinois-Indiana border; their reputation suited my own politics. Madigan seethed at the Panayotovich defection and needed this seat back to not only hold onto his Democratic majority, but to extract his revenge.

Because I lived on Chicago's north side, the campaign staff and volunteers treated me as if I'd dropped from the sky. It was unimaginable to them that I would come to their hardscrabble neighborhood of unemployed steelworkers and Superfund sites to work for their candidate.

Office manager Theresa Marzullo gave me a hilarious run-down on all the players in the Balanoff world—siblings, spouses, uncles, cousins, friends. As the campaign manager, I expected Clem, the candidate, to listen to my political advice and direction, which was filtered through the Madigan operation. When I questioned Theresa about why he always went off in contrary directions, she explained Clem was listening to his friend from grade school, or his Communist uncle from Hammond, or a guy he sat next to at the lunch counter on Ewing Avenue. Clem believed in and listened to the people. I loved that, and found managing his campaign more infuriating, more fun, and more rewarding than any political work I'd ever done.

The hilarity, heartburn and volatility of the 10th Ward's lightning-round commando politics is not what held me there. Indeed, every other day I tried to quit. As a clan, the Balanoffs are a kind and loving bunch with wide, accepting arms, loyal to the bone. Everyone who walks in the door is part of the family, regardless of color, country of origin, sexual orientation, religious affiliation, age, physical ability, prison record, mental capacity, or bank account. And I had the privilege to be in their number. We won the election, and Clem Balanoff was one of the first true progressives in the Illinois legislature. I joined Speaker Madigan's staff, assigned to Clem.

Chapter 23

My cousin Therese called me in May of 1990 to report that Agnes had collapsed and been taken to the hospital; I needed get to New Jersey as soon as possible. She fetched me at Newark Airport and drove straight to Point Pleasant. My mother was unconscious, attached to a breathing machine. I picked up her hand and noticed her freshly painted nails.

"We went for a manicure a few days ago," Therese whispered.

She'd been suffering from dementia; I'd been visiting a couple times a year. Usually we'd have dinner, go to a movie, shop. The missing brain cells must have held the carping and criticism. She was softer, easier to love, without the booze and cigarettes. Then again, her mean streak had not, apparently, diminished with others. When Therese picked her up at the nursing home for her last nail appointment, she'd heard Agnes yelling, "Get your spic hands off me!" to the Spanish-speaking attendant helping with her coat.

The hospital required all four daughters to sign a waiver in order for the doctor to detach Agnes from life. Within the week, they came. We barely spoke to each other. None of us had the mother we wanted or needed. That was sad, but her death wasn't. We were relieved.

The official cause of death states "Alzheimer symptoms due to alcoholic brain syndrome." A few years earlier, she had entered rehab and stopped drinking and smoking. But she didn't know it.

Her dementia had progressed to the point that she involuntarily mimicked both lighting up an imaginary Marlboro, and sipping an imaginary scotch-on-the-rocks. Wet brain (formally known as Korsakoff syndrome) is caused by alcohol robbing the brain of vitamin B1. This deficiency slowly destroyed her brain cells until the damage progressed beyond the point of no return, and she died.

The funeral home filled with adult versions of all the teenagers who used to call on Agnes at cocktail hour in her Jersey Shore living room. They told stories about her clever wit that often turned merciless, spiteful and mean; they all thought it was hilarious. (And it was, if your sense of humor has been seeded with East Coast sarcasm.)

She had a rarely seen kindhearted streak that manifested itself unexpectedly, as in the time she brought my three-year-old son to visit me in the psychiatric hospital. (She herself had been there every single day for 30 days.) But when I'd had emergency gall bladder surgery, she visited with her boyfriend Harry. Positioning themselves on either side of my bed, they argued the entire visit. She berated him for everything from the route he drove to the hospital, to what he ate for lunch.

("He eats his steak well-done," she said to me, as if it were an act of murder. In fact, all of Harry's life was fair game for her savage criticism—his tie clashed with his shirt, his Jaguar XKE was too flashy, he read the *Asbury Park Press*, he ate at diners, his insurance business catered to the wrong people. Whenever he told a joke she'd say something like, "I'll bet you think that's funny." Ask Harry how he could stand the constant sarcastic barrage, and you'd be met with the exact same answer, "Oh, she doesn't mean it.")

In dementia Agnes had carried an ever-present small clutch purse. She incessantly opened it and fingered through its only contents—lipsticks. The nursing home crew gave her their old lipsticks because the sound of click-clacking as she rifled in her bag calmed her down. I heard that sound my entire childhood. It haunts me.

The day she died, Therese had asked if I'd like to visit the nursing home and thank the nurses and staff. I was curious how she lived at the end. It turned out her closet was overflowing with clothes she'd stolen from other residents.

"Did she ever express guilt? Remorse? Shame?" I asked.

No, they said.

Five decades after she gave it to me, I still keep the General Electric thirty-nine-hole iron she'd bought me when my son was born. The sole is stained from those years I fell for the convenience of spray starch. Numerous falls off the ironing board onto a hard floor have blunted the tip. The faded red, white and blue settings sit atop a dulled black thick plastic handle which is wrapped with a discolored turquoise electric cord. I can still see myself in the mirror-like shine of the chrome sides. And it still works, this family heirloom.

Chapter 24

Collection agents from my father's failed coal mine wrote him off, just as he'd planned, freeing him to return home to Chicago with his wife and her small boy. But before leaving Florida, he devised another long con to replenish his dwindling funds and provide income for the balance of his life.

I had once introduced him to Emmett O'Neill, Senator Alan Dixon's chief of staff in Chicago. When he got back to town, my father asked O'Neill to secure a space in the federal building for a weekly AA meeting. Phase one of his plan was to use the Senator's address as a draw for AA members from the Loop financial district. It worked.

(This wasn't all bad. I still periodically meet people who tell me how much that meeting meant to them.

"I remember your father's meeting in the federal building. He was a big help in my early sobriety."

"He knew me better than I knew myself. Uncanny."

"Loved your father. So real. So knowledgeable."

"Told me to go to meetings and tell the truth about myself. Saved my life.")

He was not, however, practicing the principles of recovery in all of his affairs. The AA meeting served another purpose; he could now casually drop into O'Neill's office each week and talk up the deal he had cooking. O'Neil was impressed—and gave him a temporary office and phone in the Senator's meandering office suite, at no charge. *Phase One: Accomplished.*

He used the free phone line to raise awareness for his project, informing his targets he was working out of Senator Dixon's office while dropping distinctive names as if they were lifelong business partners. With his new reputation and status established, Phase Two swung into full gear: using the new connections to arrange meetings within the financial community. He had no intention of obtaining financing from the banks he visited—his was a different mark. He simply wanted powerful people to start talking about him.

How do I know all this?

He bragged about it. He was grooming me to follow in his footsteps. He relished reporting every detail of every conversation, how he fooled one into believing he knew the president of a bank, another into thinking he knew the Kennedys. And if anyone questioned his veracity? He'd viciously malign them to their own community, whether it was AA, financial institutions, business investors or friends.

When I confronted him once about a lie I heard him telling over the phone, he detonated.

"You don't trust me? You're either loyal or you're not! You're in or you're out!"

I shrank from him, but not completely. It was fear on my part. If I hadn't at least feigned allegiance to him and his plan, he might have done to me what he was doing to others, jeopardizing my friendships, and my job

When his wife left, he moved from apartment to apartment, never paying the last few months' rent. Still, his man at Gucci dressed him like an Italian movie star. He looked successful, confident, charismatic. He *was* charismatic. A friend once remarked my father's ego was so big that when Bill Burke walked into a room, he feared a wall would bust out. Face-to-face meetings were important because he looked the part, legit. As did the deal, buttressed by false implications the Senator sanctioned it, or that federal funds were forthcoming. *Phase Two: Accomplished.*

In Phase Three, my father produced a professional prospectus projecting profits in the millions for a limestone mining operation. The prospectus included the first formal photo of my father since his college yearbook, and a true-ish *curriculum vitae.* The black and white head shot showcased his large Irish face and jug ears, dark bushy eyebrows overhanging soulful eyes, and thick white hair crowning those movie-star looks. The infinitesimal upraise of one eyebrow in the photo had frightened me ever since I was a child. Lifted to its fullest, that certain tell meant a raging maniac was before you.

And now he was moving in for the kill. He and his prospectus impressed an old friend and former employer of mine, the mark: Tom Boyle.

I had worked for Tom's construction management company off and on for years. We were like family. He came to family parties and helped my son find a job. He put me on his payroll between political campaigns even though we had wildly differing political views. He dated my friends. Whenever I said I worked for Tom Boyle, those who knew him said things like: Best guy in the business. Honorable, decent, kind. I felt proud to be his friend.

Though Boyle had none himself, he recognized that most businesses had some kind of lawsuit hanging around their necks. He paid no attention to my father's questionable reputation.

The mining operation would be located in nearby Northern Indiana, and Tom Boyle was already hearing about the deal from his Chicago banker and investor friends. (All thanks to Phase

Two.) And it looked lucrative on paper. Illinois was planning a new airport on the Indiana-Illinois border; building the roads and runways would require massive amounts of limestone. Boyle agreed to provide my father with office space, a car, and a stipend. But that wasn't all: Boyle also agreed to buy the land and the mining equipment, a considerable investment. The agreement stated my father would obtain financing for the mining operation, and put his legal expertise to use towards the lengthy process of acquiring the permits necessary to mine and haul the limestone. The agreement included a fifty-fifty share of the profits between my father and Boyle.

Here's the con: the numbers my father used to convince Boyle they'd have a huge profit at the end of two years were false. He purposely understated the cost of operations. Since my father had expertise in mining operations, Boyle didn't challenge his falsified numbers. All the potential investors were cautious, though, and rejected his proposal. He knew they would; that was part of his plan. He'd heard that Boyle's family money was a bottomless pit. His plan all along was to get Tom Boyle hooked, figuring he'd eventually kick in the entire cost to run the mine.

Then came the day Boyle figured out it was all a con—that my father had fudged the numbers, and that he had no intention of securing financing. Boyle escorted him from the office, retrieved the company car and stopped paying him. *Phase Three: Failed.*

I felt like I'd been freed from a cage.

But Phase Four was yet to come.

Chapter 25

Twelve Democratic leaders and influencers were seated in leather armchairs at an oval table in one of downtown Chicago's private clubs. I was the only woman.

When Governor Bill Clinton entered the room, his tall navy-suited body seemed to shift the atmosphere, moving the dust molecules away from him and clearing the air as he moved. He gave a hearty salutation and proceeded to introduce himself to each person while he circumnavigated the room, one-by-one. I was halfway around the table, and when he reached me I stood and looked up into his bemused rosy face, full of laugh lines. He had a big red nose, like Santa Claus.

As I tried to introduce myself, he interrupted me. "I know who you are," he drawled. "You're the Executive Director of the Illinois Democratic Party. Do you know your name's the same as one of King Lear's daughters?"

"Yes," I said. "It is from Shakespeare."

"Let's keep that between us," he whispered. "She wasn't such a great character." And in that one brilliant instant, we formed a best-buddies pact. He finished working the room, told us why he was thinking of running for President, and asked us to support him. He never sat down.

A few weeks later, Bill and Hillary entered a crowded second-floor meeting room off Michigan Avenue with about fifty curious political activists who gathered to meet them for the first time. He neither ushered her in ahead of him, as a well-mannered chauvinistic gentleman would do, nor did he act like an ill-mannered boor and make her walk behind him. Side-by-side they came to us. We all jumped to our feet and cheered before he even said hello, before he shook one hand. It was two months before he announced his candidacy for president. His nascent message stressing personal responsibility for welfare recipients resonated with me. (I had no idea then that the "personal responsibility" message was something cooked up by the centrist Democratic Leadership Council. Later in his presidency I despised his welfare reform policy, but on this day I heard what seemed to me a spiritual insight that vaulted my commitment to a new height.) This was my guy.

A political acquaintance from Little Rock called a few weeks later to ask me about David Wilhelm. Clinton was considering him for campaign manager. Wilhelm was my predecessor at the State Party. He had his own Chicago-based political consulting business and worked as Mayor Daley's campaign manager. I gave David a glowing recommendation; though I'd never worked with him personally, he seemed to know what he was doing. Immediately afterwards, I called David; we talked every day on the phone after that, reporting to each other every morsel of info we could squeeze out of our different political networks.

As soon as Wilhelm got the call from Clinton, he phoned me. After the shouts for joy, he insisted I go to Little Rock to be the campaign scheduler.

It was a big question. It's the worst job in any campaign, and Clinton needed to move his presidential scheduling away from the Governor's office to the campaign as soon as possible.

"What about the women problem?" I asked. (We had all heard the rumors. It was a question even then. We all wanted to know.)

"I've been assured it's OK," he said. "I asked the same thing. They said it's been handled. There's no problem."

This seemed reasonable.

He went on: "We both know the scheduler in any campaign gets blamed for everything that goes wrong. But we'll be a good team. I need you."

The next time Clinton was in town, one of his many Chicago friends asked me to join them on the drive to Midway Airport.

We'd been at a one hundred person meet-and-greet; Clinton had learned that I'd accepted the job and was moving to Little Rock. Now in the passenger seat of the car, he looked back at me: "What did your boss say when you told him you were quitting your job?"

"He wasn't happy."

Clinton picked up the car phone, called my boss, thanked him for letting me have this opportunity of a lifetime, and said he was happy to have me on board. He ended the call by inviting my boss to bring his family down to the Governor's mansion for a weekend.

I imagined throwing my arms around his neck and kissing the top of his ever-loving head.

I was in Little Rock by the end of the week.

Governor Clinton's capitol office was abuzz with excited staff who greeted me like a long-lost cousin. His assistant briefed me on his official calendar before I headed down the street to the campaign office to my new job. It was October of 1991, and I was the first out-of-stater to arrive at the campaign. Unlike Chicago political operatives, Arkansans valued outsiders. Folks marveled that I had uprooted my Yankee life to work for their little-known candidate. My arrival was a sacred affirmation that the campaign was for real—that their guy was a contender.

The early Clinton for President campaign, unprepared for the onslaught of activity after his announcement, had hastily salvaged a hodgepodge of used desks, filing cabinets, folding tables and chairs from an old paint store down the street from the Arkansas Capitol Building. The high-ceilinged one-story space sat right at the edge of the sidewalk, as if it were a small town mayoral campaign office. I arrived to find ten phones ringing all at once, their long wires splayed haphazardly across the entire floor.

Telephone workers installed an extra trunk of wires on the telephone pole outside less than two weeks into the campaign. Inside, we added four or five phone lines every few days as more campaign workers arrived. A horde of volunteers frantically answered phones, scribbled names and numbers on while-you-were-out pink slips, and ran the slips around to campaign personnel.

Every few minutes a staffer held high a pink slip shouting, "I can't read this!"

I claimed an unused table for my desk. Pink slips rapidly piled up from people all over the country inviting Clinton for interviews, speeches, appearances, and fundraisers. New volunteers appeared every few hours. I gave them piles of correspondence to make calls expressing regrets, maybes, or requesting more information. Crowds on the street peered in the floor-to-ceiling windows at all hours. Supporters walked in for signs and buttons that we didn't have. I requested two more phones for myself, and I used all three at the same time. Working on Clinton's daily and long-range schedule for fourteen to sixteen hours a day, I barely noticed people around me.

One afternoon I saw a young man hurrying around in a nurse's uniform—white dress, tights, hat, and shoes. When he dropped off my pink slips, I asked if he had come from work. He laughed and said he was on his way to the night shift. Unlike what I was used to in Chicago, no one sneered or looked askance at our unusual volunteer.

Toward evening, my overworked eyes looked outside and saw zombies peering in. I took a much-needed break and called a friend in Chicago.

"Mark, people here seem so enlightened. There's a cross-dresser—a male nurse running around in a woman's uniform! And no one seems to even notice."

"Really? Oh, Regan. Check the date. He's in costume. It's Halloween!"

On a soft Arkansas evening in November I drove David Wilhelm and Rahm Emmanuel—then just a fundraiser—from the campaign office to the governor's mansion to ask Bill Clinton two questions: Would he accept the protection of the Secret Service? And would he make a clear statement about his stand on abortion? (Issues such as these were usually hammered out in the weeks before a declaration of candidacy, but Clinton had announced his run in early October, before he had a campaign team to advise him.)

As the campaign scheduler, I was a nervous wreck sending him to events around the country unprotected from whatever no-good crazies wanted to harm him and make a name for themselves. Federal security was not automatic for presidential candidates in the early days of a campaign, but it was available if requested, or if there were threats, known or unknown.

Women's groups were rejecting Rahm's requests for money because Clinton did not have a well-defined message on abortion. In fact, women feared he was pro-life, a death knell for a Democrat. Clinton had to commit to a pro-choice message before

Rahm lost potential campaign donors to other Democratic candidates.

In the southern mansion's parlor, Hillary was stretched out in a grey tweed suit on an overstuffed chair, with her black high-heeled feet resting on an ottoman. Blue-jeaned Bill sat in an armchair and sprang to his feet to greet us. She didn't move. Rahm and I had met her previously, but this was our first face-to-face. Serious recalcitrant eyes followed us to our seats.

I broke the ice by launching into the advantages of Secret Service protection, including the use of a secure car and agent to drive Bill everywhere he went. The meaning of the wordless message being conveyed from her darting eyes to his became clear to me as I talked: neither Bill nor Hillary wanted outsiders observing Bill's every waking moment.

I cut my spiel short, took a deep breath, asked if there were any questions.

Bill said, "We'll think about it."

In the chilly stillness that followed, I willed my racing pulse to syncopate with the ticking grandfather clock in the hallway. Rahm turned to Hillary, "Do you have anything to eat?"

Hillary Clinton is not the kind of woman who knows if there are leftovers in the fridge. She glowered at Bill, who jumped to his feet and invited us to join him in the kitchen.

As he was pulling food from cabinets and containers, Rahm explained that we needed a pro-choice statement in order to raise money from women's groups. We were discussing the complications of abortion politics when Hillary said, "Well, I am not going to stand for using legalized abortion as birth control."

In a wink our awareness shifted. We knew right then she would be deciding when her husband would have Secret Service protection, and she would be crafting the campaign's message on abortion rights.

The silent short ride back to the campaign office seemed like an endless route to a new and lonely land.

The Monday before Thanksgiving, I called my father to tell him Governor Clinton had told all campaign staff to go visit their families.

"He said we'll be super busy and out of touch from December until the end of the Super Tuesday primaries in March," I said. "So I'll be back in Chicago on Thursday. What are your plans for Thanksgiving?"

I was so caught up in the excitement of my co-workers' plans to visit their families that I'd forgotten my father never made plans to celebrate holidays. Nor birthdays. Nor anniversaries. Nor milestones of any kind.

"Dorothy doesn't want you joining us for Thanksgiving," my father said.

I had no particular ax to grind with my father's new wife, outside of her unnerving naiveté. She believed my father was going to provide a secure home for her and her son. When she'd showed me her engagement ring and asked why I didn't jump for joy that they were to be married, I'd thoughtlessly answered, "You're kidding, right?"

Like she knew what I knew.

Furious, alone, and full of self-pity, I abandoned the trip home and settled into catching up on the never-ending details of planning events, logistics, contingencies, and recruiting new advance people for my candidate. When asked, I'd lie: "I'm spending Thanksgiving in Chicago with my family." (The hunger to be normal, to be in that number, is one of my fatal flaws.)

But Governor Clinton was on to me. Late that Wednesday evening he called out of the blue and invited me to "come on over to the house" for Thanksgiving.

When I drove into the guest parking lot at the mansion, I recognized cars that belonged to staffers from the governor's office, as well as the campaign. Bill answered the door, introduced me all around, and took me into the kitchen to meet the chef. He bragged that Clarence was the best cook in Arkansas, that he was once on death row for murder, but that shouldn't scare me because he'd pardoned him.

"Thas right. Thas right," said Clarence.

People who study psychology say that, if a girl grows up craving attention from her father, she will gorge herself on various substitutes to satisfy the longing. I certainly proved that theory while stuffing myself at the Clintons' dinner table that Thanksgiving. The Governor kept telling Clarence to bring out more food. He insisted we all eat up, and my self-consciousness around overeating in public disappeared into second and third helpings.

After dinner, Governor Clinton had us all go "out back" to play touch football. I sat on the sidelines with Hillary and others. The First Lady of Arkansas laughed and joked with us about the goofy footballers, and told funny stories about Clinton's well-reported inept sports activities.

On the way back to my apartment, I stopped by the campaign office to type some final touches into Clinton's schedule for the next week in New Hampshire. Tired, but no longer angry, lonely or hungry, I took a break and called Paul Galloway in Chicago to check in. I told him about my day.

"The cook is a death-row inmate," I said, "pardoned."

"Yep. That's a tradition in all the governor's mansions in the South," Paul said.

Oh. I'm in the South.

Then I called my father and wished him a happy Thanksgiving.

Chapter 26

In January of any presidential campaign year, the candidates spend ninety percent of their time traveling between New Hampshire and Iowa, the first primary states to vote in February. In creating a schedule of events, campaigns are guided by red-hot polling data, and a candidate's time is in flux except for fundraising events which cannot be changed or postponed. Experienced campaign advance people moved from all over the country to New Hampshire for weeks at a time to volunteer for Bill Clinton before the February 18 election. Anywhere else Clinton campaigned that January, I'd call untrained friends and family and beg them to help—not easy when some barely had heard of him and (traveling expenses aside) they'd be working for free.

A few days prior to an event, the scheduler will guide the advance people through their assignments, making sure every detail is nailed down. Usually there is a whole team of advance people: Lead Advance, Site Advance and Press Advance. Advance people stay under the radar; they're often mistaken for Secret Service. Both Bill and Hillary required advance people. At one of her events, an old-time Democratic county chair asked me if I was carrying a gun; he thought I was her bodyguard.

Clinton's constant traveling companions were the Campaign Chair Bruce Lindsey and Deputy Campaign Manager George Stephanopoulos. The three of them traveled to Connecticut to a small fundraiser in the home of a well-known Democratic donor in the dead of winter.

My sister Gael lives in Connecticut; although she'd never done advance work before, and hadn't yet met Clinton, she agreed to gather him and his party at the Bridgeport airport, drive to Westport and back, and work the cocktail party.

She advanced the event by meeting with the hosts the day before and walking through their home; she'd be prepared to brief Clinton on last minute details, lead him from the driveway into the house, point out the bathroom and the telephone, and show him where he'd be standing to make his remarks. Gael called me with the names of important guests that we needed to write into the schedule so Clinton could acknowledge them. We passed items of note to the campaign researcher in Little Rock for Clinton's briefing book.

Gael and her husband rented a van, arrived an hour before the estimated time of arrival, and called me from a phone booth outside the charter terminal. We updated each other on last-minute details.

She was ready.

In the twilight of the frigid northeastern sky, Gael spotted the small plane by its tail number and walked out to the bottom of the pull-down stairs as the plane taxied onto the tarmac. She was eager to meet the future president.

After escorting the group to the van, she directed Lindsey and Stephanopoulos to sit in the far back, then put Clinton in the middle bench. Gael and her husband sat up front. Clinton leaned forward, inserted his oversized head into the space between them, and started to do his thing.

(Something about Bill Clinton compelled people to hand over their deepest darkest secrets. As his scheduler, I constantly struggled to keep him on time. He always, always stopped to listen to people.

And they loved him.)

He started with the basics of Burke family knowledge: he knew our hometown was Chicago, and asked Gael what she was doing in Connecticut. Gael proceeded to tell him more about our family on that one-hour drive than she'd ever told her husband.

Clinton touched her shoulder and told her he understood. His stepfather was an alcoholic, he said. His brother was a cocaine addict. He himself went to support groups for families of alcoholics. During the return trip, Gael, whose two children attended public elementary schools, told him her well-informed opinions about education.

I received two phone calls soon after Clinton's plane lifted off the runway.

The first was from Clinton. He said my sister was smart, that she had a lot of depth.

Then Gael called from the outdoor phone booth, away from the ears of her husband. Through chattering teeth she whispered: "I'll sleep with him anytime, anywhere."

Depth indeed.

When they returned to Little Rock, I met the plane on the dark deserted tarmac. He descended the jet's stairs with a big smile, came directly at me, grabbed my coat, and ran his extra-large hands up and down my long furry lapels.

"Nice coat, Regan," he whispered.

Governor Clinton's capitol office called me in early January of 1992 to say I had to pick a date for a man's death.

"What?" I asked. "I have to schedule someone's execution?"

The caller sympathetically explained that the law required the governor to be in the state whenever an execution occurred. There was a man on death row whose case had run its course, and he had to be put to death in January.

I shuddered to the bone. A volcano of bile rose in my belly; I barely made the bathroom before the eruption. On weak and sweaty legs, I tottered back to my office. Shaking it off, I grabbed my calendar and headed to the fundraiser's office.

"Rahm," I said, "get off the phone. This is important."

"What the fuck is wrong?" Rahm asked.

"I have to schedule a day for Clinton to be in Arkansas for an execution," I said. "So help me nail down the details of your upcoming fundraisers."

"That's great!" Rahm said. "Voters like capital punishment."

I walked back to my office and closed the door—wondering how I could possibly stay at that desk, in that office, in that job, with those fake Democrats. I picked up the phone and called Bill Clinton.

He kindly explained the case of Ricky Ray Rector, that he had wrestled with this man's story for years. He empathized with me, understood my feelings, and was sorry I had been put in this position. But as much as we don't like it, he said, it was the law, and we had to proceed.

I worked in politics my whole life, always hoping for the perfect politician. The worldview I dreamed up included good people who ultimately acted in the best interest of the whole. Bill Clinton could have been my hero. That 1992 rallying cry of personal responsibility fit in with my evolving personal quest to stop playing the victim in my own life. It was not the first, nor would it be the last time I misapplied campaign rhetoric to my private journey.

Now I had doubts. Could I work for a candidate who favored the death penalty and hesitated on his support for abortion? Those were two issues I thought every Democrat knew to be against, and for.

A young man, fresh out of college, arrived at our campaign office door in mid-January. He'd driven all night from Baltimore to volunteer for Clinton. (The rest of the senior staff was traveling in New Hampshire with Clinton, and those of us in Little Rock were fielding press calls.) I told this volunteer to go sit in the press office, take detailed messages, and tell anyone who called that someone would get back to them.

The next day, the kid came to me flushing from head to toe, barely able to talk.

"Someone called and said there's a story coming out about the governor having an affair."

Oh no. Not again. I need to find a place to stay in Chicago. Herb & Vivienne? The Galloways? Maybe I'll go to the Bahamas.

"Get your notes. We're going to call George, and you're going to give him every detail."

I knew at once we'd need more advance staff, a bigger plane and security, just like we did when this happened to Gary Hart five years before. The supermarket tabloid *Star* released the story about Gennifer Flowers and Clinton on January 23, 1992.

Clinton's small plane touched down in Arkansas.

Ricky Ray Rector died by lethal injection on January 24, at 10:09 pm.

The Clintons appeared on *60 Minutes* two days later to say Flowers was lying.

The next day, Gennifer Flowers held a press conference releasing tapes of phone conversations between her and Clinton.

The scheduling office had three scheduling desks and one travel coordinator who handled the plane tickets, hotel reservations, and rental cars for all the advance staff, Bill and Hillary Clinton, their traveling staff, and the traveling press corps. After the Gennifer Flowers expose, the office was a madhouse. We had no time to interview and hire new people. We shouted to each other over ringing phones, broke into tears and laughter, individually and collectively at any odd moment.

On February 18, Bill Clinton came in 2nd in the New Hampshire primary and proclaimed himself "The Comeback Kid."

The phrase "personal responsibility" disappeared from the campaign rhetoric.

"This is not your fault," James Carville said in that red-hot Cajun voice of his. "I take full responsibility."

It was rare to get a phone call from the chief campaign strategist in early March. He was trying to take the fall for a scheduling incident. I knew right then the campaign staff on the road with Bill Clinton were blaming me.

A few days earlier, Carville had directed me to schedule Clinton at the Stone Mountain Correctional Institution in Georgia, a boot camp for young male prisoners. The strategists reasoned that a photo of Clinton strolling with black inmates and Southern white male politicians would cinch Clinton's appeal to the state's (white) Reagan Democrats, and he'd win the upcoming Super Tuesday primary in Georgia and six other Southern states.

I assigned an advance team for the hastily organized event. One of them called me a few hours after he'd arrived and had gotten the lay of the land.

"Regan, the Ku Klux Klan hold an annual cross-burning at Stone Mountain Park. Are you sure you want Clinton to come here?"

Bill Clinton's New Democrat campaign advisors—the conservative wing of the party—were determined to make him the law-and-order candidate. When I questioned Carville about the site, he assured me the bold move would boost our poll numbers. The photo on the front page of every paper in the South won Clinton several primaries, but not without a price. The national press excoriated Clinton for his racial insensitivity.

Democratic candidate Jerry Brown said, "Clinton and the other politicians looked like colonial masters trying to tell white voters 'Don't worry, we'll keep them in their place.'"

And, as predicted, it was the scheduler's fault.

The person who plans a candidate's calendar has an enviable yet risky position. An unfortunate photo in front of Hooter's? Protesters blocking the entrance to an event? A rained out rally? The candidate misses their plane? The scheduler gets stabbed in the back, and the front. The Clinton campaign, more than any place I'd ever worked, filled up with self-promoters, finger-pointers, blamers and blamees. The campaign manager stopped defending me, and I had neither the time nor inclination to figure it out on my own.

At the end of every grueling sixteen-hour-day I felt like I'd been pelted with unripened tomatoes. Placating the enormous Clinton network was as time-consuming as strategic scheduling. I could never figure out who to listen to. Sleep was constantly interrupted by phone calls from aggressive Friends of Bill's (FOB's) who questioned me on every move he made—everything from who introduced Clinton onstage, to what sandwiches were in his holding room.

Typically, the calls came after the FOB's had all talked to each other late at night and designated someone to set me straight.

Often I'd answer the phone and hear ice tinkling in a glass on the other end.

"Hey! Did you order flowers for his holding room? Don't you know he's allergic to flowers? He came out with puffy eyes. What's the matter with you?"

"Who approved (some local politician) in the receiving line? He's married to my cousin and is a disgrace to the family."

"Don't you know he doesn't eat tuna fish? Turkey sandwiches. Everybody knows that."

"What's with that advance guy? He brought his family to the fundraiser and spoiled the ambience."

"How come he was late? You forgot to build in more time for city traffic."

Campaign operations temporarily moved from Little Rock to Chicago's Palmer House just before the Illinois-Michigan primaries on March 17. The extensive Chicago staff in Little Rock wanted to celebrate Clinton's anticipated nomination-clinching St. Patrick's Day victories in our hometown.

Matthew Baio (a former co-worker, loyal friend, and Chicago policeman) volunteered to use his vacation time to be Clinton's driver during the few weeks he campaigned in Chicago. Matt called me at two in the morning the weekend before the primaries.

"Regan! That Greek guy and Bruce Lindsey were'n the backseat tellin' Clinton you have to go."

"What?"

"Yep. But Clinton said he wansta make sure you get another high-level job in the campaign."

"Really?"

"Yeah! These guys are strategists? They're talkin' 'bout firing you in your hometown—and your buddy drivin'?"

We howled at the strategic blunder. Then we discussed where I'd work when I returned home to Chicago.

After the Illinois and Michigan primary wins, the press proclaimed Bill Clinton the presumptive nominee. Back in Little Rock the campaign shifted to general election tactics and started gearing up for the Democratic National Convention in July.

Campaign Manager Wilhelm asked me to be the convention manager. I knew of three other people who thought they had that job. When I asked if he was signaling me to leave the campaign, Wilhelm shrugged.

The New York Times was reporting I'd been replaced before I'd even had time to pack my bags.

Chapter 27

I'm not exactly sure what a nervous breakdown is. Is it the same as a mental breakdown? Emotional breakdown? Whatever it's called, I've had a few of them. Like, in every job I've ever had. And with every man I've ever loved.

I told Wilhelm I was leaving—not much response there. When I told my co-workers, I shook uncontrollably. I retreated to the Bahamas, became achingly lonely, and returned to Chicago. Outwardly I blamed getting canned on sleep deprivation, instead of my frazzled emotional state. I didn't want to admit physical, mental and spiritual collapse.

When I left Little Rock, Herb and Vivienne Sirott settled me into one of their apartments in their downtown high rise. Vivienne and her daughter accompanied me to rescue a Scottish Terrier from the basement of Carl's Junk Store in Uptown. We called him Voter. Herb thought dogs were the same as wolves. He said we build walls to keep wild animals from invading our homes. But he knew I needed this.

One day Vivienne and I were cooking up some kind of Lucy-and-Ethel scheme in her living room when we heard thumping in the hallway. Herb was kicking a tennis ball down the hallway for Voter to fetch. Herb thought Voter the smartest animal in the world and played fetch with him every day after that. Voter became obsessed with tennis balls. He'd dig at cans of them behind closet doors and find unrecognizable ones under every bush surrounding the tennis courts at Lake Shore Park. After veterinarian Dr. Gross failed at saving seven-year old Voter on the operating table, she brought me the cause of his death. Hard bits of green fuzzy rubber broke through his intestines. Tennis balls.

The newly elected Cook County Clerk, David Orr, hired me as Deputy Director of Elections. We worked to boost voter turnout and voter registration culminating in passage of the National Motor Voter Act. A young community organizer, Barack Obama, walked into my office at the end of the summer to ask for my help in planning a county-wide voter registration project. Things looked good from the outside, but inside ego-busting despair maintained constant watch over my soul.

The elevator opened to a lit-up scene of human statues in the closed-for-business City Hall lobby.

"Cut! Close that elevator door!"

I slinked back into the elevator, up to the 4th floor Elections Department and flew to the telephone in my office where, in the Saturday morning quiet, I had completed the 1993 Cook County Election Day plan.

I called Vivienne.

"You have to come down here right now!"

"Ach. Can't possibly. Bogged down. Writing," said Vivienne, a frustrated nine-to-five insurance executive who spent her weekends grinding out movie scripts.

"You must. They're shooting a movie in the lobby. We can get access with my ID."

Vivienne and I loved sifting through the credits at the end of movies trying to figure out what everyone did. We had watched movie and TV crews shooting scenes all over Chicago, but we'd never been on a real movie set.

Chicago's City Hall squats on one city block with doors on each street. I hurried to the Washington Street side of the building down the stairs to the lobby. Flyers were posted in the stairwell: Lobby Closed Saturday Noon for Filming of *The Fugitive*. When did they put those up?

I ran down the hallway, shoved open the polished brass doors and caught my spirited, garrulous sidekick swinging her long legs out of a taxi on Washington Street.

Vivienne's knockout looks never suffered from uncombed hair and no make-up. Flinging her camel-hair cape over her shoulder she shivered in the March wind, grabbed my arm and skipped inside. I muttered quick instructions: don't embarrass me, don't say a word, don't make me laugh, do not get me in trouble.

Crew Only signs sat on food tables along the corridor. Perched at the table near the rotunda we hawk-eyed bowls of popcorn. Vivienne whispered her intuitive movie-credits knowledge.

"That's the Director," she pointed, "the production assistant. There's the Script Supervisor."

"Which one is the Grip?"

"Dunno."

A crew member gestured to the popcorn, assuming we were extras. Vivienne helped herself. *What? Don't do that!*

Action! Harrison Ford came running down the circa-1911 polished marble staircase across the wide rotunda zig-zagging through the crowd of extras I had witnessed by the elevators. Cut! He walked back upstairs. Action! He came running down again chased by Tommy Lee Jones.

Cut!

"Oh my god, he's coming this way. Vivienne! Say something!"

Harrison Ford sauntered over to munch popcorn. I shoved Vivienne toward him. He said hello and she asked him how he liked Chicago.

"Is that an Irish accent?"

"'Tis."

"How do YOU like Chicago?"

"Love it."

"Well, I love popcorn." He smiled and strolled away.

My starstruck legs wobbled. Back at my side with a handful of popcorn, Vivienne shined. Turning toward the exit we faced crew and extras gathered for the catered lunch behind us.

"Are you two extras? What's that ID around your neck?"

We skedaddled down the hallway, fluttered out the doors and whooped it up all the way home.

I had tucked the shirt of my mental collapse into my skirt presenting myself every workday as an emotionally stable, confident, experienced political operative. Eventually depression, isolation and shame undressed workplace effectiveness and led to naked suicidal thoughts. I cracked up again and took an extended sick leave. I slept, walked Voter, ate ice cream and laid on the couch staring at the ceiling, planning how to kill myself. I feared walking beyond a two-block vicinity of my building. Nearby AA meetings would have loosened my chained-up spirit but I choked every time I tried to talk. I went to the eye doctor complaining I couldn't see. There was nothing wrong with my vision. To every person who phoned, I simply said, "I'm depressed."

Vivienne brought a psychiatrist friend of hers to my apartment. She sat on the couch and I in a chair but she was too far away to talk to. I couldn't get my words to reach that far. She gave me Prozac, my first legal anti-depressant.

About that time I received a call from a Chicago friend who was working in the White House Personnel Office. He had the perfect job for me in the Department of Education and asked if I was available to move to Washington. I accepted without deliberation, convinced God was lifting me out of the bottomless sinkhole I'd accidentally tripped into. It was a sign. God's will.

Chapter 28

Cognitive dissonance: "In psychology, cognitive dissonance is the mental stress or discomfort experienced by an individual who...is confronted by new information that conflicts with existing beliefs, ideas, or values."—Wikipedia

I moved to Washington to work as Secretary of Education Richard Riley's scheduling director.

During the campaign Dick Riley—a former South Carolina governor—had turned his whole life over to help elect fellow southerner Bill Clinton. Riley's gold-standard reputation for loyalty, kindness and political wisdom led Clinton to select him as head of the presidential transition team, then name him Secretary of Education. Riley and Clinton had worked on education issues as members of the Democratic Governor's Association; South Carolinians called Riley the "education governor."

(I once asked Dick Riley what he considered his greatest achievement. He said in the fourteen years he sat as a legislator in Columbia he set about to systematically dismantle South Carolina's Jim Crow laws, and got through most of them. When his tenure in the Clinton Administration was complete, *Time Magazine* named Richard Riley one of the 10 best Cabinet Secretaries of the twentieth century.)

Secretary Riley's decision to hire me was influenced by the simple fact that I was from Chicago. A wily as well as honorable statesman, Riley assumed experience in Chicago politics gave me the mettle necessary to withstand the numerous hoodoo scheduling proposals that plagued his staff, particularly from White House advisor (and fellow Chicagoan) Rahm Emmanuel.

Rahm's bullying, intimidating tactics gave Chicago a bad name in the Clinton Administration. Yes, Chicago politics is hardcore, but the one characteristic that identifies all Midwesterners—friendly—was never on display in Rahm. He racked up policy points as a sycophant of the Democratic Leadership Council, a centrist think tank that powerful Chicagoans like Jesse Jackson rebuffed as "Democrats for the leisure class." Bill Clinton had been the Chairman of the DLC before becoming President. And though Clinton truly was friendly, he accepted Rahm's hard-charging profanity-laced personality because he thought America needed (or maybe wanted) Rahm's right-of-center ideas.

In deference to his New-Democrat roots that required him to be tough on crime, Clinton passed the Violent Crime Control and Law Enforcement Act of 1994. This bill expanded crimes that were eligible for the death penalty; it also included a "three-strikes" provision requiring life in prison for two or more previous violent or drug trafficking convictions, and created incentives for states to build more prisons. There were admirable aspects of the bill— banning assault rifles, for example—but every political friend I had opposed the abhorrent provisions. It wasn't just that we feared the bill would lead to future mass incarceration for young black and brown men—that was a given—it was that the policies smacked of a moral failing. They were dead wrong.

Next, Clinton signed the North Atlantic Free Trade Agreement, NAFTA. Labor union friends fought against NAFTA for fear U.S. manufacturing jobs would move to lower-wage Mexico. I joined protests by environmental groups who demanded NAFTA's anti-pollution provisions be made stronger. Both of these loyal Democratic groups lost their battles over NAFTA.

These and other neoliberal policy shifts were spearheaded by Rahm Emmanuel, who decidedly did not have the public good at the forefront of his self-serving mind. I despaired.

Disillusionment and distress settled in the space around my bones and muscled me awake at three o'clock in the morning every damn night for seven years in my tiny DuPont Circle garden apartment.

I should add that tensions with my father had finally come to a head shortly after my arrival in Washington. Remember his coal mine scheme? The unplanned phase—Phase Four—had taken a little while to wrap up.

All along, I'd known only the details my father revealed, enough to know he was up to no good. My friendship with Boyle had been damaged, but at least the deal no longer spun around endlessly in that what-do-I-do corner of my mind.

Then my father did what every experienced con man does: he assumed the role of victim. He constructed a false narrative and phoned everyone he knew to report how Boyle had cheated him. Next, he filed a lawsuit—for breach of a financial agreement with an elderly person.

Illinois had passed an elder abuse law, the Adult Protective Services Act, in 1988. My father zeroed in on the particulars of the new law and discovered all he had to do was prove he was over sixty years old, suffered from a physical impairment (heart disease), and that Boyle had breached a fiduciary relationship.

That did it for me.

I called my father from my office in Washington, begging him to drop the lawsuit.

"Stop trying to scam money from my friends. Stop it! Right now!"

"You don't know what you're talking about! I won't stand for your disloyalty," he screamed into the phone.

Disloyalty. Connivers always deflect from their own vices by accusing others. I'd never accumulated any money of my own, and I'd depended on him for help with living expenses well past the time I knew better. He threw all of that in my face—all the money he'd spent on me, the time he'd helped me get sober, the husbands he'd saved me from, all of it.

Before he hung up, he added one last torment: "I'm going to bury you."

I didn't know what he meant at the time, and he may not have known either. It didn't matter. The aftershock of that seismic emotional blast broke all the dishes in my internal cabinet. The damage was irreparable.

I sent Boyle an affidavit describing the details of the conversations my father had had with me and others about his plans to defraud Boyle. It was damning. I expected the affidavit to stop the suit in its tracks. But no.

Instead, my father added me to his lawsuit. He used the witless idea that I'd schemed with Boyle to steal his project. He did what I'd always feared. He phoned my sisters, my son, my boss, and mutual friends; he raged against my disloyalty, saying I was probably sleeping with Boyle (I wasn't) and getting a lot of money from him (I wasn't).

We never spoke again.

I poured myself into my work. It seemed like something I could control, at least.

A lobbyist for Siemens International contacted me frequently inviting Secretary Riley to visit one of the company's innovative programs in Lake Mary, Florida. Siemens provided on-the-job training for students at Lake Mary High School. The program exemplified President Clinton's school-to-work policy, and I put it on a list of possible events for the secretary.

Rahm, then the Assistant to the President for Political Affairs, decided a big flashy event highlighting Clinton's School-to-Work Opportunities Act before the 1996 reelection campaign would score points with Reagan Democrats. He asked Secretary Riley for suggestions. Riley consulted me, and we chose the Siemens/Lake Mary partnership.

Since I'd be organizing and managing all the details for the President's visit to Lake Mary, I was immediately posted to the White House's scheduling office. I tiptoed into my first day on the detail as if I'd wake a sleeping giant who'd shout, "You don't belong here!"

Within the first few hours at my desk in the White House, I received a call from a colleague at Education. He'd uncovered some unseemly intelligence—Siemens had collaborated with Hitler.

Uh-oh.

I immediately reported this to the President's scheduler. She hastily called a meeting of decision-makers and sent me with others to an afternoon meeting with Deputy Chief of Staff Harold Ickes and Rahm. These two were known for hurling f-bombs right at your face before you even sat down. ("Who the fuck are you?") Life in the fray of Chicago politics conditioned me for profanity, but these brawlers took it to another level. They were famous for not only sparring with each other, but also lobbing the most obscene and demeaning sucker punches at ringside innocents.

Rumors were rampant that each of them offered outsiders access to the president in exchange for campaign contributions. My Nazi information put the Lake Mary event in jeopardy which, in turn, meant a potential lost opportunity for big campaign cash from Siemens.

The meeting participants rat-a-tatted around the room on the pros and cons of going or not going. Their only concern: What would the press report? My quivering lips involuntarily clamped shut. Participation in this conversation would have been like throwing myself in the ring with Muhammad Ali.

I finally blurted out: "They had a factory at Auschwitz."

Heads turned and I felt dragon eyes spit fire in my face. My cheeks ignited.

"Are you saying we shouldn't go?"

I knew my answer would either shorten or prolong my envious seat in a White House office.

"I'm saying Siemens helped fund the Nazi party and later used prisoners to work in their factory inside Auschwitz."

They all decided it was too risky for President Clinton, and that ended my eight-hour post in the West Wing. Secretary Riley was happy to have me back. He had a sense that I'd get eaten alive "over there at that White House."

One sweaty August morning in 1995, NPR told me Jerry Garcia died.

I collapsed on the bathroom floor weeping. At 49 years old, my idealism had come to an end. Disillusionment in the Clinton White House, the collapse of my plastic world of everlasting good: these things felt complete with Jerry Garcia's death. Reality glared back at me in the mirror as I brushed my hair, seeing for the first time a wrinkled face and rubbery neck. I dressed in a soft yellow cotton frock and pinned a silk flower in my hair, ready for the grieving day.

Voter squirmed away from my extra-long hug and I headed out the front door. My old friend Keith Lesnick was waiting to drive me to work. As soon as I buckled my seatbelt, the tears returned. He asked what was wrong, and I slobbered out a few words.

"Jerry Garcia signed into rehab last night," I said. "He died in his sleep."

Keith waited a few respectful minutes, then said, "Well, it's not as if it's Aretha Franklin."

My quicksand fall instantly found dry ground. Comedy has always been an interim salve for my diseased psyche. With that one simple sentence, Keith had reminded me of that unspoken caveat to much of life: *don't take yourself so seriously.*

Chapter 29

The First Lady celebrated her fiftieth birthday with a private party at the Chicago Cultural Center in October of 1997. Chicago transplants working in the Clinton Administration were not only invited to the party, but were invited to fly with her and Bill and their guests aboard Air Force One from Washington.

Per instructions, I joined my fellow Chicagoans a few hours prior to the scheduled take-off in the 1950s-era lounge at Andrews Air Force Base outside Washington. Boarding the plane in a heightened mood, we located our assigned seats in the guest section in anticipation of the arrival of the Clintons and their friends.

They all arrived in a motorcade from the White House. Senator Barbara Boxer sat down next to me. Ted Danson and Mary Steenburgen sat in the two seats facing us. I sent a "thank you" text from my pager to my friend in the White House who had compiled the plane manifest and assigned the seats.

Mary Steenburgen is an old friend of the Clintons. She and Ted had married about a year before. Ted looked nervous and self-conscious. I knew he had a hair transplant or plugs or something, and I couldn't take my eyes off his scalp. Mary chatted away, making introductions and jokes, and we all relaxed. As soon as we were in the air, Bill Clinton sauntered back to the guest section. He introduced me to the two movie stars, then told them that I had worked in the campaign in Little Rock. They acted impressed. I felt impressive.

We landed at O'Hare in thirty-nine-degree rain and rode downtown in the presidential motorcade. I rushed to the makeshift staff room to use a secure landline because cell phone coverage failed inside the nineteenth century cement landmark. My son was at my father's hospital bedside, and I needed to call.

I had neither seen nor talked to my father for years.

"He just died," Joe said. "Do you want to see him?"

"No. I'll call you later."

I looked at the only other person in the room, a Secret Service agent I didn't know.

"My father just died. He's in a hospital five blocks down the street."

"Oh, I'm sorry. Are you leaving?"

"No."

I wandered down the hallway to Preston Bradley Hall, grabbed a Diet Coke, and walked around in a daze, nodding to old friends. I found Bob Sirott, who had a morning news show. Bob and I had arranged to talk off the record about what it was like to ride on Air Force One. I described the inside of the plane, and the food, and gave him a box of M&M's imprinted with the aircraft's seal.

I left early to overnight at Joe's apartment. He told me some bits and pieces about my father's last hours. Joe had been his grandfather's caregiver at the end, fully aware of the demons and secrets and empty bank accounts that still surrounded the embittered seventy-nine-year-old.

"There's a will," Joe said.

"I doubt there's much left."

As it turned out, his will called for the distribution of his remaining eighty thousand dollars to six people: my three sisters, Joe, a long-forgotten girlfriend, and me. I gave my split to Joe, who was starting his own family. He deserved far more for all that time he'd spent as caretaker of an unforgiving old man, all the time he'd spent listening to his grandfather constantly demean and diminish me.

Up in the air the next morning on a United flight back to Washington, the cumulus heaven below held me in silent contemplation. My mantra: thank God he's dead.

His Shakespearean patrimony echoes ancient tribal legends and informs modern family feuds: icing out the enemy, the silent treatment. (It's the preferred weapon of narcissists, and a common one for the Irish.) He turned into King Lear, pitting my sisters and I against each other in his madness. He convinced each of us that we weren't worthy of the others' attention. And it worked. There's been scant communication between us since.

His greatest legacy smolders from the grave, in the feeling we struggle with between each other, and towards him: silent scorn.

Chapter 30

I needed a break. So, too, did my colleagues. It took a few months for four of us—Rocco, Kristina, Mark and I—to organize our jitter-filled lives around a two-week vacation in a thousand-year-old fishing village in Cinque Terre on the Italian Riviera.

We left the nineteenth century train station in Vernazza and rolled our overstuffed suitcases for twenty minutes up a cobblestone switchback twined in purple morning glories. Our home abroad sat thirteen hundred feet above the Mediterranean Sea and overlooked a village of a thousand happy Italians. We arrived at LaTorre midday, when the sea is dark turquoise and the sun swells the nose-tickling lemon and olive trees.

(LaTorre is a thirteenth century pirate lookout with a galley kitchen, a modern bathroom, a luminous living-dining area, and an alcove captain's bedroom. Three other beds are lofted into stacked platforms in a stone tower, and the only way to get to them was by rope ladders. We negotiated our sleeping arrangements and headed back down the path to the village.)

Like bloodhounds we followed the scent of ground basil and garlic around the village into a ristorante on the piazza at the harbor. Our first meal was homemade bread dipped in fresh pesto, Vernazza's culinary legacy to the world.

In the days following we hiked the village-to-village trail along the sea, returning to Vernazza by water taxi. Other days the train took us to Le Spezia, Portofino, Pisa, and Lucca. At night we lounged on LaTorre's heirloom terrace in front of the twinkling lights of passing boats on the navy blue horizon.

Then the phone rang.

One of my fellow staffers at the Department of Education crackled on the phone line frantic to let me know that a journalist was about to call me wanting information about Monica Lewinsky. He recommended I consult with a lawyer before taking the call. Our perfect vacation bliss was now teetering on a cliff over a darkened sea.

In the spring of 1997, I'd been asked by the White House to take a few hours from work to advance President Clinton at a small fundraiser in a Washington hotel. An old friend from Indianapolis came into the room through the metal detectors following Monica Lewinsky. Twenty-two year old Lewinsky had a reputation among advance people as a Clinton stalker. I asked my inexperienced Hoosier friend to shield the President from her clutches if Clinton happened to pass by her while shaking hands along the rope line after his speech. This was a common practice among advance people—protecting Clinton from intrusive and potentially troubling women.

A half a year later, news had broken about a grand jury investigation into Clinton's relationship with former White House intern Lewinsky. In Indianapolis, the Hoosier friend panicked that he would be hauled before the grand jury. Eager to inoculate himself, he held a press conference describing his brief encounter with Lewinsky—and mentioned my name, which is how my vacation got interrupted by inquisitive reporters.

The sudden jolt of reality stirred our *La Dolce Vita* quartet to hatch hilarious mad scenarios to confound the soon-to-be-intruding journalist. In the end, when the call came, Rocco simply answered. *"Prrrronto! Si? No Inglese! Ciao!"*

Che finito, we returned to our *intermezzo* between the acts of the crazy world.

Back in Washington, I consulted with a lawyer, who assured me he'd do for me what every Clinton staffer wanted—and keep me out of Independent Counsel Ken Starr's investigation of President Clinton. And so he did.

A few months later, I ended up on a Department of Education trip to Barcelona.

My colleagues and I vowed to take time between our official duties to squeeze in a meal at the celebrated El Motel restaurant in Figueres, ninety miles north of Barcelona

An international business consortium had invited Secretary Riley to speak on the importance of public education at their annual conference in the Palau de la Generalitat de Catalunya. I arrived a week before the Secretary to arrange the logistics for the two-day conference, and for the Secretary's visit to a Catalan school in the nondescript dusty countryside between Barcelona and Figueres, whose principal had formally (and serendipitously) invited Riley to visit. The school children celebrated Riley with an unscheduled performance of an original musical play of American tunes. It added hours to our day. With official business out of the way, we headed for the Salvador Dali Museum in Figueres. My colleagues and I stewed around the museum in anticipation of a late lunch at the table of chef Jaume Subirós.

Dali said of his museum, "The people who come to see it will leave with the sensation of having had a theatrical dream." At first glance the entrance looked like a quaint three-story red clay castle. Looking atop the turret one could see huge cement eggs. The exterior walls were peppered with what looked to foreigners like baked dinner rolls. (Catalonians know the scatological Dali created the organic sculptures to resemble excrement pies.) The aphrodisiacs inside included Dali's surrealistic art, holograms, a vintage interactive Cadillac and his crypt. We frittered away more time than planned, and in the end found Secretary Riley and his wife resting in the Mae West living room.

Drenched in Dali elixir and blanched by a long day without sustenance in arid Catalonia, we made our way north on the Avenida de Salvador Dali, away from the theatrical dream and toward the gastronomical paradise of El Motel. The U.S. consulate in Barcelona had booked our table, and we were greeted with all the ruffles and flourishes of royalty. Parched from tongue to stomach, we dragged our low blood sugars to a round table full of tea roses and peonies overlooking the windswept Spanish countryside. *Yes, yes!* We agreed to start with plates of Iberian ham. And ice water. Other shared plates would dish up seafood croquettes, rice with sea cucumbers, rabbit and sausage, clams with candied tomato & lemon grass. The chef had prepared fresh Catalan custard for dessert.

As the Iberian ham was placed before me, I jerked up in horror to see Secretary Riley turning beet red, struggling to breathe. The table sprang into emergency mode. Someone called an ambulance. We deserted our anticipated delights and followed it to the Figueres hospital, where Riley and his wife ended up staying overnight as he recovered from an asthma attack.

In our Barcelona hotel the following day, we were comforted with simple ham and cheese sandwiches before leaving for the airport. Secretary Riley, a perfect Southern gentleman, apologized to us all for the disappointing trip to El Motel.

Chapter 31

As part of the White House Advance team, I had traveled to Birmingham, England in May of 1998 to help with President Bill Clinton's schedule during the G8 Summit. At Clinton's behest Russia had become a member of the group the previous year. (A privilege which was suspended in 2014 because of their annexation of Crimea). Assigned to make arrangements for Clinton's bilateral meetings, I'd learned his meeting with Russian President Boris Yeltsin was my most important duty. It had to be discreet, secure and comfortable.

For ten consecutive days before the summit began, I tried to meet with my Russian counterpart at their headquarters hotel. Instead of civilians, the Russians used officers from the FSB—the successor to the KGB—for their advance teams. (Our Secret Service generally didn't commit resources until these meetings were scheduled by the White House advance team.) Even though the press speculated Boris Yeltsin was too ill to attend the G8, the U.S. pressed the Russians hard to schedule the bilateral meeting as a show of Russia's support for the latest nuclear non-proliferation agreement.

We got word at the last minute that President Yeltsin would meet President Clinton upon the former's arrival at the Russian headquarters hotel, twenty-four hours after the start of the G8 summit. That prompted the FSB to finally admit me to the secure floor of their headquarters.

(When there's a big conference going on, like the G8 summit, the ballrooms and big conference rooms are used for the public events, so the various governments need to use hotel rooms for their working spaces. Everyone needs their own secure communications equipment and wiring, so the governments often negotiate with the hotels for months ahead of time to remove walls and pay for the reconstruction afterwards. And the hotels—eager for the publicity they get from hosting these events—are happy to oblige.)

As I exited the elevator and entered an open door at the end of what would have been a typical hotel hallway, I faced men and women sitting at long tables stretched the entire length of the floor. The hotel rooms' walls had been removed, and tangles of wires dropped from the exposed ceilings to telephones, fax machines, computers, cameras, and ominous electronic components. I announced my name and asked for my contact.

The nearest of the twenty-five or so Russians laughed out loud. "We know who you are," one said.

You do?

Wide-eyed at the cornucopia of visual information, I gawked at the long stretch of FSB agents wearing headsets and staring at video screens. One ferret-looking guy strutted around, glancing over the others' shoulders. My Russian contact approached, and we proceeded to the room on the mezzanine reserved for the off-the-record meeting between the two heads of state. I called my Secret Service counterpart, and the three of us performed our obligatory walk-through, agreeing to the safest route for both presidents through the hotel, with enough exposure for the media to observe the two men strolling casually together.

The day Boris Yeltsin arrived in Birmingham, he fell down the stairs getting off the plane and was carried to his car. His FSB aides helped him into the hotel elevator, but he lumbered on his own down the exposed hallway to greet Clinton. My job completed, I left for the staff room in the U.S. headquarters hotel, where I saw a televised report that Yeltsin appeared inebriated, and suggesting that the two leaders may have had a less-than-fruitful conversation.

I met the Russian team once more, a year later in Auckland, New Zealand during the 1999 Asian-Pacific Economic Cooperation summit. Though Russia is not a part of APEC, Prime Minister Vladimir Putin—a little-known former KGB agent who'd only been appointed a month before—flew to Auckland that September to secretly meet Bill Clinton. I secured a space and told the Russian team when and where to bring Putin. When I briefed President Clinton on the logistics of the clandestine meeting, he told me Putin was a real bad guy. I asked why he was meeting him. Clinton said he was going to succeed Boris Yeltsin as Russia's president.

I led Clinton to the undisclosed site and saw Putin for what I thought was the first time. Later in the staff room, it struck me that Putin had been the Russian puppetmaster in that room in Birmingham the year before.

Boris Yeltsin had a reputation for public drunkenness and erratic behavior. Foreign service officers casually speculated that Putin kept Yeltsin plied with vodka and drugs to render him ineffective, hoping that Yeltsin, who had a known heart condition, would either be forced to resign, or drop dead.

Back in Russia, Yeltsin retreated to his presidential dacha outside Moscow. Rumors flared that he was too sick or too drunk or too drugged to carry on. When he resigned in December, he appointed Vladimir Putin as acting President, as predicted.

Chapter 32

Living in Washington D.C. and working in the Clinton Administration should have been a dream come true. But when I wasn't working in the office or on the road, I was hiding in my apartment. Some of my colleagues at the Department of Education held my same political idealism but I judged other commuters rushing back and forth to their government offices each day as very different from me. Men and women dressed alike—dark suits, poly-cotton shirts and unpolished shoes. Entry level political appointees were nipping at everyone's heels, itching to swoop up better jobs. That's all a depressive like me needs—to be paranoid about who I talk to and what I say for fear of losing my job.

I found solace in the sea, frequently visiting relatives at the Jersey Shore and in lower Delaware. Aunt Joanne lived in Bethany Beach. Everyone in Washington will tell you it's a two hour drive. It always took me three. If I was lucky enough to have Joanne to myself, she'd take me sightseeing around the Eastern Shore; we'd go on nature walks and look for blue herons.

An old boyfriend called to say he was in Washington on his book tour. He asked if I'd meet him at the Mayflower Hotel. We hadn't seen each other since high school. A lot had happened since then. I told him I'd walk, that the hotel was near my place.

"I know."

Dammit. How did he know where I lived?

The last time I remembered being with him was in senior year, when he showed up out of nowhere at my high school. We had been involved the previous summer in a whirlwind beach romance consisting of sex and well, sex, and sex.

Before he'd returned home for Labor Day, I'd told him my love for him had faded. He had killer good looks, but his only interest was body-building—his and mine. By then I had already read Camus and De Beauvoir, was a full-fledged alcoholic, and liked to converse in existential gobbledygook. We had little in common.

But there he was, at my school, preening with desire to show me his new car. He sweet-talked the school secretary into pulling me from French class.

We drove around and eventually ended up at his parents' beach cottage. He'd promised them he'd check the pipes, something people with summer houses always seemed to be doing.

Inside the cold, boarded-up house he pressed his six-foot pumped-up frame against me at the kitchen counter. I squeezed out from under him, furious at myself that I'd gotten in such a predictable mess.

"Oh, c'mon, just kiss me. I know you love me, don't you?"

The fear of succumbing to this wooing from a man I didn't like rose up in me as if I'd come face-to-face with a bear in the woods. I had to get out of there.

"Don't you have to check the pipes?"

I flew out the door as soon as he was out of sight, and ran down the boardwalk to a fisherman's bar, a place I often ended up at in the early morning hours after drinking all night. Fumbling around in my pocketbook for a coin for the pay phone, I yelled to the bartender for a draft, then called a friend to come get me. I hid in the ladies' room with my beer until she arrived.

And here I was, twenty-five years later, walking into the Mayflower to meet him.

I called him from the lobby phone.

"C'mon up," he said.

"No."

"Oh, c'mon, I have to get ready for my TV interview. Nothing's going to happen. I promise."

I laughed when he told me I still looked good despite the weight gain. Figuring my middle-aged corpulence might be enough to dial down his testosterone, I nonetheless refused his offer to have a seat on the bed.

"Why did you call me?" I asked.

And why the hell was I there?

He wanted to tell me he'd published a few books, and it was all because of me. When I'd broken his heart, his English teacher had advised him to write about it. He'd written every expression of real and imagined tortured love, details of everything we'd done on the beach and in the basement of his cottage that summer. He confessed that after I'd spurned him repeatedly, he'd taken my sister out and screwed her for revenge. Guilt and shame squeezed itself into every cell of my body as he talked.

"You really did love me, didn't you?"

"No."

"Aw, yes you did. Look at me! Don't I look good? Look at these muscles? I've been taking steroids to bulk up."

As he pulled on his tie he bragged he'd also been using estrogen-reducing Tamoxifen to keep his breasts from enlarging.

I asked about his latest book. It told the story of a detective hunting a serial killer. The chase led to an underworld of illicit bodybuilding drugs, sadomasochism, rape, and sex trafficking.

Walking home alone in the twilight, I felt inflamed membranes surge under my skin. I vowed to never respond to calls from old boyfriends again. The next day I saw autographed copies of his book prominently displayed in Kramerbooks on Connecticut Avenue. The cover was ghastly. Thank God I was only the muse.

Secret Service protection of Bill and Hillary Clinton stepped up during Clinton's second term. Agents insisted on "covered arrivals." If either of them were to arrive at a building entrance with a line of sight from surrounding buildings, the Secret Service erected a tent over the outside entrance to shield them from sniper fire, and public view. The public saw less and less of them waving as they exited their limousines. Scuttlebutt among advance people led me to believe viable threats to the Clintons' lives had escalated.

The Secret Service safeguarded the President and First Lady, not advance people. If bullets started flying, no one would be throwing me to the ground behind a bulletproof limousine. I was on my own, scared to death on every advance assignment with Bill and Hillary.

A Chicago friend keeping watch over my umpteen nervous breakdowns tried to warn me. He said moving to Washington was not a sign from God, that it wasn't a good move, and that the job and place were killing me. I stopped talking to him.

My default modus operandi is self-sufficiency. Deep inside my soul grows a bed of weeds whose dandelions of reason attract me like nectar to bees. Reason tells me I am my own master gardener. I provide my own seeds, water, nutrients, and sun. Reason tells me it's unnatural to ask for help, or to accept advice from others. Participating in AA meetings had helped me disrupt that hardened self-centered God complex, but I'd stopped attending AA. My physical, mental and spiritual condition slid closer to hell every day.

Back-to-back overseas trips, with their attendant jet lag, exacerbated my chronic insomnia and triggered flu-like full-body pain episodes. A doctor diagnosed fibromyalgia; he said there was no cure, and no medication I could take. He told me to get some sleep, reduce my stress level, and stop traveling. I walked the dog less frequently, and laid on the couch for weeks at a time, uselessly chugging down over-the-counter pain relievers. Eventually I put someone else in charge of my job and moved into another office at the Department of Education, hoping no one would bother me. I reasoned that since we were in the last months in office, I had to archive Secretary Riley's papers.

All spiritual teachers say a life lived on reason leads to despair. During the last year of the Clinton Administration, I visited a psychiatrist, Dr. Canaan, every day of the week. Each morning I'd drive across the Potomac to his office in northern Virginia and pray I'd not break off into Walmart, buy a gun, and blow my brains out.

An old friend from the Gary Hart campaign met me for lunch while I was on sick leave and inquired about my condition. I told him I was afraid I was going to kill myself or someone else, but I was under the care of a good shrink.

A few days later Dr. Canaan got a call from someone in the Department of Education's Human Resources Office asking if my security clearance should be revoked, barring me from the building, because I'd threatened to kill someone. Dr. Canaan told her I was sick, not dangerous. He cautioned me about telling the truth about myself to anyone in Washington.

"Don't trust anyone," he said, "Someone's always out to get you in this town."

Dr. Canaan helped me navigate through the tidal wave of emotions at the closing of the Clinton era and the beginning of the George W. Bush administration. Despite my opinions about Clinton's centrist policies, I admired him and Hillary enormously, believed they loved the country as I did, and was grateful to have had such full experiences. I sold my condo to one of the hordes of happy Republicans who flooded my neighborhood. Dr. Canaan cautioned me to take an easy job upon my return home to Chicago, find a therapist, and travel only for vacations.

Chapter 33

I threw down the Sunday Real Estate section, flew out the door, and sped toward the city to catch the tail end of an open house in a downtown condominium. View of Lake Michigan, one-bedroom, nine hundred square feet, twenty-four-hour doorman, close to everything, dogs allowed, balcony.

Balcony? During the hour-drive from temporary quarters in my son's suburban home, I fantasized sitting on the as-yet-unseen balcony overlooking the Lake, tending my potted garden.

"I'll take it," I said to the agent as soon as we made introductions at the threshold of the third-floor apartment.

Across the room, outside the wall-to-wall windows, I saw old-growth trees half dressed in their spring clothes. A red-headed house finch hopped from limb to limb. Then, there was the balcony.

Before light bulbs, blinds, or even a new shower curtain, I bought clay pots and flowering plants. I had the screen door removed to have no obstruction to the outdoors. I imagined young lime green sweet potato vines and purple morning glories growing up hugging each other, curling around the railings, stretching toward the sun, competing for space on the top rail, then spilling over the top, and finally hanging down in a cascade of tangled color.

I laid the pots of soil on the balcony overnight to let the dirt cure before planting, leaving the door open, inviting overnight breezes to induce a soft sleep. In the morning I strolled into the living room to find dirt tracked all over the floor. Usher, my new one-year-old Scottish Terrier—legs splayed out on the balcony floor, muddy nose, dirty paws—held his head high with half-closed eyes basking in the light wind. What do you suppose dogs think? Was he grateful I gave him the opportunity to dig up our new backyard?

Off to Home Depot I went for another bag of soil and over-the-railing brackets to hold the pots up and away from those ancient digging instincts. I planted and watered. Perfect.

My north-facing building juts out enough on Chicago's North Lake Shore Drive to have a tree-filled view of Lake Michigan. Those trees are all that stand between my balcony and the North Pole—no buildings, no mountain ranges, not much to break the full force of north winds barreling down the over the Great Lakes, slamming into my balcony and battering the sweet potato vines and morning glories. They didn't last the week.

For three years I tried all manner of perennials and annuals, praying for wind resistance. The gardeners at Gethsemane Garden Center finally told me I was in a losing battle. Abandoning the outdoor garden, I settled for the delight of a tree-filled panoramic view full of sparrows, chickadees and starlings. A lone squirrel sat on a parallel branch, squeaking and shaking his tail, tormenting Usher.

Eventually the emerald ash borer brought down most of the old trees, allowing more light to fall on the indoor geranium garden I spread across the window sills. Protected from nature's wrath, they bloom all year.

On cloudless Saturdays in the early aughts, I'd slough off my dead weekend chores—grocery shopping, haircut, laundry—in favor of the beach. I filled my backpack-chair with a bottle of water, mosquito spray, dog treats, a beach umbrella, *Vanity Fair*, and a small purse.

I strapped the chair to my back, gripped Usher's leash and walked across Michigan Avenue through the bee-buzzing garden leading to the Oak Street Beach underpass. I hurried past the watery underground restrooms, holding Usher tight to keep his nose off the ground. We climbed the cracked cement stairs to the maniacal bike path that gripped the edge of the beach.

During mid-week Junes, Park District beach workers would be spending early morning hours bulldozing clean sand over the previous winter detritus. Seagulls argued over the gleanings, anticipating the arrival of their human garbage dumpers.

Usher and I would dodge the slipstream cyclists and jump down into the sand that swallowed up the sound and stench of the Lake Shore Drive traffic. We'd set up shop at the shoreline. I'd face my chair away from the sun to protect my ultra-violated skin, screw the umbrella to the armchair, and settle in with my magazine. Usher dug into the sand under my chair and rested. As the beach turned to follow the sun, I'd stretch, take Usher for a swim and reposition my chair.

Nearly every week I'd have lunch with a friend on the shady deck of the Beachstro Cafe. The hamburgers were lousy. But we sat with our backs to the skyscraping neighborhood, at the water's edge, hearing nothing but the lake licking the sand and seagulls singing over the water.

We might as well have been on a Bahamian island.

One day the lifeguard rushed over to me on the beach, "Get your dog out of the water! Don't you see the red flag? No swimming. E. coli. It'll make your dog sick."

E. coli is a nasty bacteria that causes stomach disorders—the last thing a dog owner wants for their little housemate. I packed up immediately, ran home, and gave the poor guy a thorough bath.

Chicago beaches are tested for e. coli every day in the summer. In the early 2000s, high concentrations showed up regularly, indicating a saturation of fecal matter. DNA studies showed the e.coli landed on the beaches from seagulls and washed into the lake.

Huh? It was in the sand, too?

The press reported there was a twenty-four-hour delay in test results so at that time, when a beach closed due to water contamination, it meant we had been exposed the day before. The Chicago Park District solved the problem by hiring border collies to chase the gulls off the beach.

Oh, the border collie! The smartest worker in dogdom. She doesn't simply chase the gulls. She crouches down and makes eye contact as she creeps toward her prey. This terrifies the gulls and they fly off. When the birds try returning to the sand they face the same threat; the collies never get tired. By instinct these dogs won't catch or bite the birds, an important point since gulls are still protected under the Migratory Bird Treaty.

My beach days were over the day the collies started shooing away the gulls. Usher didn't mind, but I was constantly reminded of bacteriological threats. I've found watching the lake from the crazy bike path is as idyllic. No medication can replicate the blue serenity of Lake Michigan. It is its own anti-depressant.

Chapter 34

Throughout '02 and '03 I'd been raging against the Iraq war, often rallying under the fire-orange Calder sculpture at Federal Plaza hanging hope on words, sometimes from Reverend Jesse Jackson, sometimes from local organizers, and sometimes from State Senator Barack Obama.

"I'm not opposed to all wars. I'm opposed to dumb wars," Obama told us.

In March, after the U.S. bombed Baghdad, I scrummaged up North Lake Shore Drive with ten thousand irate activists steeling ourselves against the Lake Michigan hoarfrost. Mayor Daley wanted no disruptions to the shoppers on the Magnificent Mile, so when we turned west toward Michigan Avenue, the police herded us into a group on Chicago Avenue. Troublemakers were handcuffed and hustled out of the crowd into police buses. My grey hair and full-length down coat disguised the revolutionary boiling inside me. I was not singled out. I crossed Michigan Avenue and watched from the sidelines before walking home to ice my smoldering knees.

Secretary of Defense Donald Rumsfeld, whom Richard Nixon once called "a ruthless little bastard," had been a key architect of the war. By the end of 2006, he'd resigned, battered by controversy over the torture of enemy combatants, and accused even by his generals and officers in Iraq of poor military planning and strategic incompetence.

Then one Sunday he showed up at my church.

I'd been a member of the Presbyterian church since 1984. I'd been on a soulful search for a place where God shared an unbuttoned space with the intellect. I had exhausted myself in eastern religiosity, women's Bible studies, spiritual communities of light and love, and the emotional squeeze of evangelical Christianity. And then my friend Paul Galloway told me I'd like Pastor Elam Davies at Fourth Presbyterian Church. "He's a great orator," Paul said.

Davies' exegeted sermons always distilled into one message: love God, love your neighbor. And now Donald Rumsfeld, a fellow Chicagoan, was my neighbor, sitting alone in the pew in front of me under the pulpit at Fourth Presbyterian Church.

I had never seen him in church before, but I knew he was a member. Everybody knew. Church members had wanted him thrown off the rolls, banned, shunned. Pastor John Buchanan, a true statesman who had denounced the Iraq war in every sermon, once had to announce to the congregation, "Donald Rumsfeld is a member of this church, and that's all I'm going to say about it."

All through the service that Sunday I fumed, formulating what I would say to Rumsfeld after the closing benediction. Perhaps I'd ask him if he regretted what he did, or perhaps I'd ask how many civilian deaths he was responsible for. I settled for one word which I intended to deliver with samurai precision, swift and deadly.

Buchanan stepped down from the pulpit as the service came to a close. He didn't stand at the center to recite his usual benediction. He came over to Rumsfeld instead, greeted him with a handshake, and quickly escorted him towards the side exit.

I half rose from my seat; I wanted to chase after him with a clenched fist, sputtering: "Murderer!" But he got away.

A young pastor at church formed a group one summer to study the bestseller *Jerusalem: A Biography* by historian Simon Sebag Montefiore. He wanted to gauge the analytical capacity of his flock using a sliver of the congregation. Twelve souls signed up to explore the chronology of the Holy City.

The two-hour monthly gatherings were ably guided by the intellectual pastor, but ensuing discussions broke down as participants looked at the ancient past through the lens of the present. At one of these sessions, we were discussing a ruthless, manipulative ruler of ancient Jerusalem when a woman in my group said, "This reminds me of that candidate who talks all the time about her disabilities to gain sympathy votes in her run for Congress."

"You mean Tammy Duckworth?" I replied. "The helicopter pilot? The one who was shot down in Iraq and lost both her legs?"

"Yeah, that one," she replied.

Church is a messy place. I never feel like I belong, and I never call myself a Presbyterian.

I call myself a Christian. I love the same Jesus whose friendship saved me when I was a child. I trust that my despair, my depression, my addictions and my character flaws don't change the universal goodness of God. I've been saved from the insanity of self-will over and over, against all human odds. AA shows me there is a power greater than myself. None of us alcoholics or addicts could possibly walk into the doors of a twelve-step program and ask for help on our own. It's simply unnatural. Our natural state is un-sober. But I have a higher power that is neither punishing nor retributive. Not to me. Not to others.

I go to church seeking an explanation, even a replication of spiritual experiences I see in AA, but my soul is never satisfied.

Still, I keep going. Pastor Davies told me the universal Christ is bigger than I can comprehend. I know that. I've seen it in the life of Tammy Duckworth.

This female war hero got out of her healing bed and jumped into the psychological warfare of politics. After she lost her first run for Congress, she told us she sat in her bathtub for three days and cried. *Yes*, I said. *This is the real deal.* She's even fearless in her vulnerability.

Tammy won her second run for Congress representing suburban Chicago, then went on to be a U.S. Senator. Her two artificial legs enable her to stand erect at podiums on the floor of the Congress and at public events. She chases after her small children in her wheelchair. *Where does she get such courage, such stamina, such otherwordly resilience?*

I need these reminders and examples. I continually need to be told to love my neighbor, otherwise I would haul off and slug people—like the woman in the book group. Or maybe Donald Rumsfeld.

Chapter 35

My friend Llani O'Connor and I were Hillary Clinton fans during the 2008 Presidential primary season. We constantly exchanged did-you-hear-what-she-said exclamations all through the summer and fall of 2007 after she announced her candidacy.

I had been Hillary's advance person on a few trips. I never failed to be completely starstruck by her brilliance, kindness, and sense of humor. In back hallways and holding rooms at events, Hillary insisted on surrounding herself with local event organizers and their families. She listened to people's problems and laughed at their jokes. Then she'd deliver a detailed speech on a complicated issue without looking at her notes. Llani and I were ecstatic to be alive for the first woman running for President. We knew she was going to win.

We obtained three tickets after I shamelessly begged an old friend on Hillary's staff. Our third companion Jeanette, a native of England, drove us down State Street, dodging and weaving and ignoring stop signs and red lights, crossing over Lake Shore Drive and then barreling back north to Soldier Field's south parking lot.

It was a sunny ninety-one degrees in Chicago that afternoon, outside the stadium. We had hats and water but everyone arrived at four for a seven o'clock start time and the stadium walls offered no shade. Fifteen thousand of us thumbed our noses to the heat as we danced around and sang songs waiting for the big event. After that wild ride, Llani and I were feeling lucky to be alive

We rushed into the stadium onto the field to get the closest seats possible. The stage was set at the fifty-yard line, with long red, white, and blue panels hanging behind it from overhead rigging. Dark blue curtains hung behind the panels, blocking the field and stadium seats behind the stage. Folding chairs filled up the rest of the field.

We snapped a photo once the event started; it shows us with sunny smiles and blouses opened to our bra-lines—red-faced, droopy-haired and sweaty. In the distance we see all seven candidates, a full fifteen months before the election: Chris Dodd, John Edwards, Bill Richardson, Joe Biden, Dennis Kucinich, Barack Obama, and Hillary Clinton. (Who was way ahead in the polls.) The moderator, Keith Olbermann, joked that if the candidates didn't behave he'd cut off their (obviously non-existent) air conditioning.

When the ninety-minute forum ended, we waited for the candidates to leave the stage before heading to the car for the treacherous ride home.

Then: "Llani! Hillary's out in the audience shaking hands. Let's go!"

We plowed through hot bodies and upturned chairs, eager to get as close to our hero as possible. All of a sudden Llani climbed onto a folding chair and took off, hopping from one chair seat to another, camera in hand, screaming at Hillary to look her way. I bent over laughing at the sight of her in baggy pink linen shorts, purple sneakers, and sleeveless turquoise tank top, teetering on chair after chair to snap photo after photo.

After that rush, riding home with Jeanette and going the wrong way down one-way streets at sixty miles an hour was anticlimactic.

Chapter 36

In Genesis, Cain groans in pain after being ostracized for killing his brother. The medical community recently caught up to this storied ancient idea and identified the "silent treatment" as a factor in chronic pain. After our father died, Maere crowed that I was too fat and poorly dressed to be in her family; she never spoke to me again. Those talons are forever embedded in my aching bones.

My family's Irish-American heritage is awash with feckless silence. When my mother moved my sisters and I away from our pre-teen suburban Chicago home, my parents had stopped talking to each other. Judy Collins once said Irish Alzheimer's is forgetting everything but the grudges; we'd moved to the coven of Irish Alzheimer's—the Jersey Shore. My mother's relatives stopped talking to my father, and my sisters and I weren't allowed to talk to him, either. And when I rebelled at sixteen, packing my bags and running off to live with my father, he wouldn't allow me to talk to my mother. For a while, Maere called often, and even came to visit. My father bought her a Cadillac in a shallow display of love. After that, she returned to controlling our relationship with the silent treatment.

My father never talked about his relatives. I had no idea his sister had children until his niece, my first cousin, contacted me on Facebook when we were in our sixties. She revealed that my father occasionally tried to finagle money out of her mother. In between these schemes, he didn't speak to his sister for years at a time. Observers of my father often armchair-diagnose his legerdemain life as narcissistic. I don't know about all that. I only know that he spawned some kind of bad magic in his family.

When the memory of being ostracized re-enters my consciousness, every aching sinew yearns for my family. Gael and I were good friends into adulthood, until I unknowingly offended her; she, too, succumbed to Irish Alzheimer's, and I've spent the last few years enduring the silent treatment.

Irish DNA also seems to have a gene predisposed to alcoholism, although there's no clear scientific evidence that it's hereditary. My parents' chaotic, calamitous alcoholic marriage intruded on the childhoods of my three sisters and I, but as far as I know my siblings are not all alcoholics. We all manifest common characteristics of growing up in an alcoholic home: fear of emotions, conflict avoidance, perfectionism, compulsive behavior, depression, melodrama, overreaction to change, and the denial of all these traits. (And denial of their connection to alcoholism.)

In the decades I've been in Alcoholics Anonymous, ongoing questions and discussions persist. Is it hereditary? Is it a disease? Since the 1900s the language describing alcoholism has screamed out to the non-addicted populace, WE CAN'T HELP IT. The world has been given plenty of messages to allow acceptance of alcoholics as normal people with medical problems. Currently, the community that studies these questions is promulgating the idea that addiction is a biological disorder from a dysfunctional brain—not inherited, and certainly not a moral failing.

In casual conversation at coffee hour after a Sunday church service an acquaintance told me she had a first date who told her he was in AA. "Isn't that disgusting?" she said.

Alcoholism was shameful before I was born, shameful in my family growing up, shameful in myself, and shameful now. All the work that has gone into trying to change negative thinking against alcoholics has not shifted the stigma. Two million recovering alcoholics still sneak off to life-changing, life-saving AA meetings, keeping their recovery a shameful secret.

Agnes died of alcoholism when she was seventy. Bill joined AA when he was forty-five and stayed sober until his death thirty-five years later. He thrived on the attention from AAers; it made him feel like some kind of AA guru, which in turn propelled his ego into a whole new dimension. People mobbed him at meetings and called for his help. He had all the answers and was always right. But he never felt comfortable in the world outside the AA fellowship. He simply could not hold his own in the modern social or business world, as if a cloud of old ideas followed him around. He wasn't secretive about his alcoholism; nonetheless, the stigma hounded him until the end.

Chapter 37

In October 2016, my friend Susan Keegan hopped into her shiny red Cadillac with me, and we booked out of town to Ohio.

Our mission: canvass voters for the Hillary Clinton campaign. Ohio was a battleground state, and we had friends to accommodate us in the lead-up to election day.

Our canvassing territory was Ohio City, a quaint restored section of downtown Cleveland. Thirty-eight hours before we left town, the Chicago Cubs had won the World Series against the Cleveland Indians. The final game had taken place in Cleveland; conscious of the seriousness of our mission, we vowed to keep our Cubs hats at home. I even told someone I was from Toledo to offset the anticipated antagonism.

We met old and new friends —Keith Lesnick in from Sonoma, Carol from Washington D.C., Jamie from Oakland, Dennis from Virginia and even Vivienne Sirott (or Decourcy now, after Herb's death), who flew in from Ireland in the effort to nail the Trump coffin shut.

News from my iPhone said Chicago's victory parade for the Cubs would be held the next day; it would start at Wrigley Field and roll down Lake Shore Drive to Michigan Avenue to Grant Park—heading right past my condo building on the way. "Oh Noooo," I groaned, "I'm going to miss it." "Do you want to go back?" Sox fan Susan asked half-jokingly. *No.* It felt like God's work. *No turning back.*

I texted my nineteen-year-old grandson Charlie and told him to go to my place to watch the parade. He'd already been planning to bring his brother—ten-year-old Jerry—into town from their suburban home to spend the night and get a good position on the parade route. "Thanks for letting us stay," Charlie texted. And when they got there: "Jerry borrowed your Cubs hat. Hope you don't mind."

By the time Susan and I arrived at Cathy and Marc Dann's vintage Tudor outside Cleveland, we were exhausted from talking the entire seven-hour drive about Hillary's winning campaign. All the polls said she was going to win. The betting community said she was going to win. Astrologers said she was going to win. The last time the Cubs won the World Series, the incumbent party won. Since Hillary was the incumbent party's candidate, we took that as one more sign. We were about to have our first woman president. After the Cubs last won the World Series in 1908, it was another twelve years before women were allowed to vote. We'd won the pennant with Hillary in 2016. This election was our World Series.

It was four days before election day. Susan, Vivienne and I grabbed our assignments at the Hillary volunteer office and took off to nearby neighborhoods. Cleveland's fall colors were in full bloom during the sunny sixty-degree days as we knocked on doors and talked to voters. Everyone was for Hillary. Everyone was going to vote. Some had already early-voted. Life was good. We were winning.

From my third floor balcony in Chicago, Charlie and Jerry each took iPhotos and videos of the Chicago Cubs open air buses with the players, their families and friends, team managers, coaches and owners as they crept down Lake Shore Drive onto Michigan Avenue. Cubs first baseman and cancer-survivor Anthony Rizzo lifted the trophy above his head as fans shouted, "We Never Quit."

At the election night party in Ohio City, the first bit of bad news came over the TV: Indiana Democratic Senate candidate Evan Bayh lost. Wizened political operative Keith flashed a guttural look, "That's bad."

Fourteen hours after the polls closed in Cleveland, Susan and I drove home. We had no trophy, no win, no good news. But we vowed, like the Cubs and their fans, to never quit.

Years before, when I returned from my neurotic stint in the 1992 Bill Clinton campaign, a psychiatrist had treated me as if I had Post-Traumatic Stress Disorder. Within weeks of that visit, Hillary Clinton visited Chicago to speak at a women's forum. I stood alone in the back of the room, away from the crowd. Someone came to me and said Hillary wanted to see me backstage. She greeted me with a teary hug, said she was sorry I'd left the campaign, and asked if I'd consider working at the Democratic Convention. I told her I was too tired, that I wouldn't survive. She understood, thanked me for all I did to get the campaign off the ground, and assured me her door was always open. We parted as friends, equals. When I later worked in the Clinton Administration, I saw her many times. My admiration for her superior intellect increased, always sweetened by her unscripted and genuine kindness toward me.

I felt a thousand little cuts during the 2016 campaign, watching her withstand the cruelest name-calling and ugly attacks—not only by her opponent but by my own friends. For months after the election I felt like she'd died, like I'd died, like the country had died.

At the end of that bleak November, I looked out the window over my MacBook Air, watching three crows bounce from bare tree limbs to the ground and back—cawing to each other about their Thanksgiving dinner. I believed they knew me, saw me looking at them. They restored me, enlarged my soul, allowed gratitude to seep in. (If nothing else, I was grateful for them.) I wondered for the millionth time since Election Day what Hillary was doing.

All of a sudden, something popped up in the corner of my screen: "White House Forced to Reverse Course on Trump's Golfing." I instantly broke off communing with my wild pets and opened the link to this urgent story. I don't dislike golf, but I'm not interested either. However, I had involuntarily begun to relinquish my time to so-called breaking news. I clicked. The next thing I knew a little box appeared with a photo of a pair of shoes I coveted. *Hmmm, I wonder if those are on sale.* I clicked.

As I lifted out of my chair to take a break, I saw two pop-ups I had to read first: "Is a 'Deep State' Subverting the Presidency?" and "Bald Eagle Population Booming In Chicago."

This compulsion, this savage addiction—it's my sentence for latching on to the fantasy that something was going to happen to reverse the outcome of the 2016 election.

Chapter 38

On the Platte River in central Nebraska I gathered with friends from Chicago for the spring migration of the Sandhill Cranes. We arrived at our cabin in time to hustle down the way to the Audubon Rowe Viewing Stand at the river's edge. There we parroted the hundred-odd birdwatchers on the stand, steering our binoculars toward the goose-like honking in the sky. The cries grew louder and the first wave of cranes appeared. Thousands of birds swirled in the overhead vortex down into the shallow river with their spindly feet splayed like landing gear on an airplane. It took over two hours for the birds to land in their overnight roosts on the sandy Platte. We pressed our binoculars into our eye sockets until every last bird nudged itself into place, snuggling alongside its friends in the water for the night.

The long-beaked crimson-headed North American Sandhill Crane coexisted with dinosaurs, making it one of the world's oldest bird species. For six weeks every spring, 600,000 of these five-foot-tall grey beauties stop in Central Nebraska.

At dawn, Peter, Amy, Anne, Laurie and I made our way back to the riverbank on Elm Island Road for the lift-off. The cranes yakked each other awake in one of nature's most melodic cacophonies. After socializing until mid-morning, large groups flew off in waves. Others foraged in the corn fields adjacent to our cabin, packing in calories for their long trip north.

Murmuring overtook the viewing stand. Our nature-loving brood—from Illinois, California, New Jersey and Florida—grew collectively quiet to hear the cranes' every cackle, trill, and honk.

"I was in Jersey once. Drove out route 80 to 70 to 35 to the Atlantic Ocean."

Why do men always talk in numbered roads?

I overheard an Audubon tour guide whisper on down the line to her group, "Right there, below that white roof at the river's bend, there's a whooping crane." I focused my binoculars.

There it is.

There are five hundred whooping cranes in the wild in North America. I ran to my pals at water's edge, squeezed my binoculared arms tight to my chest, repressing a squeal, "There's a whooping crane!" We were silenced by the stark white ladle-shaped body of the whooper shuffling among the blue-grey hordes of Sandhills that stretched over a mile upriver. We reported the news to strangers around us, lending our binoculars to latecomers, cooing when the big white bird stretched its wings in view of our naked eyes. I whispered to Peter and Amy, "If I see a river otter before we head for home you can throw me from the plane, because my life will be complete."

An hour later Peter nudged me, "There's an otter." Fishing around in the water, diving down and popping up, nature's graceful pet latched onto a tangle of twigs and leaves, twirling around and around as it floated downstream under the bridge away from sight.

Yes, something happened on the Platte. *Was it you, God? You, who are both doubtable and certain? You, the everlasting instant?*

(I am thinking, perhaps, of the hymn "You, Lord, Are Both Lamb and Shepherd" aka "Christus Paradox," by Sylvia Dunstan; she drafted these words on a commuter bus "after a particularly bad day at the jail" where she was serving as chaplain:

You, Lord, are both Lamb and Shepherd.

You, Lord, are both prince and slave.

You, peace-maker and sword-bringer of the way you took and gave.

You, the everlasting instant; You, whom we both scorn and crave.)

I suspect looking to the past to explain the present is a natural phenomenon, one we've used to nail each generation's stake in the Oregon Trail of human history. It seems we cannot escape the age-old pull of looking for what we have in common with those who've gone before us.

When I first saw my first-cousin Barbara in Omaha—where I passed through on my way to the spring migration—she shouted, "Oh my God, you look just like Grandpa!"

I had been eager to meet her, eager to learn still more about who I am and where I came from; I was hungry for Barb's memories about Grandpa and our other relatives, the Kilroys. There were a few similarities in the dead forebears, but none of it compared to Barb herself: a fellow rabid Democrat who loves Hillary, cultivates indoor geraniums, adores her Scottish Terriers, rides her bicycle, and has art-covered walls. Her yard is full of birdhouses and flamingo planters.

Barb told me our grandmother's name was Katherine. Because she was killed in a car accident when my father was a toddler in Terre Haute, he had never known her. My father was the type who kept secrets; he never even mentioned her name. And yet my son, despite having no knowledge of his great-grandmother's name, named his own daughter Katherine. My father's father, whose looks I favor, had a girlfriend, Stacy, whom my father secretly visited in Indianapolis in the fifties. My father named his youngest daughter Stacy. My mother couldn't have known the connection; she would never have stood for naming her baby after anyone connected to my Midwestern father. Barb disclosed that most of my father's relatives were not the drinking type. (Perhaps it was my mother's choice we never met them. She found non-drinkers the ultimate in lower life forms. The only thing lower: Midwesterners.)

I keep looking for some ancestral typecasting to blame for my body shape, my alcoholism, my arthritis, my murderous thoughts. But Jesus and Buddha both teach us that we are who we are in the moment, unyoked from the past or the future. Practicing this spiritual axiom requires me to act against all my ancestral instincts. Living in the moment—mindfulness—is the foundation of my physical and mental health. I tend to the *everlasting instant* in AA meetings, listening to the manifestation of a Higher Power in unrehearsed nowness falling from the mouths of the recovered. I practice *now* words there. What's happening now. Today. In the moment.

Chapter 39

One hundred and seventy days into the Trump Administration, I flew to an annual board meeting in Washington of a national anti-sexual-violence organization. Lively meals with D.C. relatives, the board meeting itself, and coffee afterwards with former political cronies old-shoed me into a comfortable and safe frame of mind. Still, our conversations sometimes veered into anxious thoughts—fears about the danger to come, and the danger that surrounded us. We were, after all, in the nation's company town, Trump's ground zero.

I arrived at National Airport an hour early for the non-stop flight home to Chicago. Packed with fellow travelers, pop-up sunglass vendors, maintenance workers and airline personnel, the terminal sizzled. I managed to nudge a stool into a space at a long table rigged with outlets, plugged in, and nose-dived into the computer-news rabbit hole. *Click.* Trump crashed a wedding at one of his resorts. *Click.* A sinkhole had formed in front of Mar-a-Lago. *Click.*

Annoying conversations buzzed around my ears: something about a hazmat incident at the control tower. *Click.* Local TV stations report fumes from roof construction at the Leesburg control tower have shut down all flights for four airports around D.C. *Click.* I suspected the Trump crowd were capable of every dirty trick in the book: *Is Steve Bannon trying to terrorize us? Did he sabotage the timetable to turn the screws on some disagreeable Administration insider?*

The announcement came: "We don't know when flights will continue. We'll update you as soon as we know." It was ten o'clock when I learned my flight was cancelled until the next morning. The United gatekeeper shouted out to the stranded throng that all the hotels were booked for fifty miles around, and that maintenance crews would be handing out blankets for those who'd be sleeping in the airport. No problem, I'd contact one of the five people I know in D.C. and ask to lay my aching bones down on a couch. *Click. Click.* All five were non-responsive. Travelers were staking out their spots on the floor.

I tottered up to the desk and shook my cane at the gate attendant: "I cannot sleep on the floor! Can't you see I have arthritis? Is there no other solution?"

He shook his head.

"How much would it cost to get to the nearest hotel?"

"Fifty miles away? About a hundred dollars."

"Oh, no! Are you giving vouchers for cabs?"

"No."

I was dragging my bright orange canvas carry-on away with no hope of a reprieve, doomed to slump to the floor by Dunkin Donuts, when a young man came up behind me and pressed something in my hand.

"Please let me help you. Take this," he said, before disappearing into the crowd.

A hundred-dollar bill. Before I could even shout "Thank you!" my Facebook Messenger app lit up with a query from Dan Murray, a consultant who'd helped us at the Cook County Elections Department over ten years before.

Click.

"FB is telling me you are nearby! Can I see you?"

And right then, I was no longer afraid I'd die.

Click.

Click.

Click.

Epilogue

I write these truths at my window from an old high rise anchored to Potawatomi land in downtown Chicago. Henry the dog sits at my feet as I spy on crows cawing around the trees rooted to the Lake Michigan shore.

Writing the truth has cured the physical pain from spinal stenosis.

Telling the truth has cured the emotional pain sprung from lifelong feelings of not belonging.

Because true belonging only happens when we present our authentic, imperfect selves to the world... – Brené Brown

About the Book

A unique hybrid memoir, Regan Burke's *In That Number* chronicles one woman's struggle to find grace and peace amidst the chaos of politics and alcoholism. It's an important public book from a longtime Democratic party activist, one whose beliefs led her from protesting the Vietnam War at the Lincoln Memorial to working inside the White House—a woman with fascinating firsthand reminisces about everything and everyone from Woodstock to Vladimir Putin, from *The Exorcist* to Bill Clinton, from Roger Ebert to Donald Rumsfeld. It's also an intimate and revealing private memoir from a woman who spent a harrowing childhood being raised by shockingly dysfunctional parents—a roguish naval-aviator-turned-lawyer-turned-con-man father and a racist socialite mother—and bouncing from house to house to luxury hotel, trying to stay one step ahead of the creditors. (And not always succeeding.) It's an entertaining and ultimately heartwarming journey, from private schools to the psych ward, from hippie communal living to the corridors of power to the pews of church, and through the rooms of twelve-step recovery to the serenity of long-term sobriety.

About Tortoise Books

Slow and steady wins in the end, even in publishing. Tortoise Books is dedicated to finding and promoting quality authors who haven't yet found a niche in the marketplace—writers producing memorable and engaging works that will stand the test of time.

Learn more at www.tortoisebooks.com, find us on Facebook, or follow us on Twitter @TortoiseBooks.

CPSIA information can be obtained
at www.ICGtesting.com
Printed in the USA
LVHW110104311020
670157LV00006B/312

9 781948 954129